SIMPSON bob

The reasons why

SIMPSON bob

The reasons why
A decade of coaching, a lifetime of cricket

with Terry Brindle

To Michael
We were Friends
when we met.

Bob Simpson

HarperSports
An imprint of HarperCollins*Publishers*

Harper*Sports*
An imprint of HarperCollins*Publishers*

First published in Australia in 1996
by HarperCollins*Publishers* Pty Limited
ACN 009 913 517
A member of HarperCollins*Publishers* (Australia) Pty Limited Group

HarperCollins*Publishers*
25 Ryde Road, Pymble, Sydney NSW 2073, Australia
31 View Road, Glenfield, Auckland 10, New Zealand
77–85 Fulham Palace Road, London W6 8JB, United Kingdom
Hazelton Lanes, 55 Avenue Road, Suite 2900, Toronto, Ontario M5R 3L2
and 1995 Markham Road, Scarborough, Ontario M1B 5M8, Canada
10 East 53rd Street, New York NY 10032, USA

National Library of Australia Cataloguing-in-Publication data:

Simpson, Bobby, 1936- .
Bob Simpson the reasons why: a decade of coaching,
a lifetime of cricket.

Includes index.
ISBN 0 7322 5664 X.
1. Simpson, Bobby, 1936- . 2. Cricket - Australia.
3. Cricket - Coaching - Australia. 4. Coaches (Athletics) -
Australia - Biography. I. Brindle, Terry. II. Title
796.358092.
Printed in Australia by Griffin Paperbacks, Adelaide.

9 8 7 6 5 4 3 2 1   00 99 98 97 96

Contents

To Meg,
Without whose support, love and devotion anything that I may
have achieved in life would not have
been possible nor worthwhile.

And to all my cricketing mates, for all the enjoyment and pleasure
they've given over the years.

Foreword
by the Prime Minister, John Howard

I witnessed Bob Simpson's first Sheffield Shield innings for New South Wales against Victoria. He was then only 16 years and 11 months, next to Ian Craig, the youngest person ever to play first-class cricket in Australia.

Forty three years on, he is still a household name in Australian cricket. No-one has had a more active involvement in the game over a longer period of time.

Bob Simpson reached the pinnacle — Captain of Australia — more than 30 years ago, yet in many respects his influence on Australian cricket in recent years has been as great as when he actually was the skipper on the field.

A very classy opening batsman, a champion slip fielder and a more than competent leg break bowler; these were the individual skills which combined to make him such a formidable cricketer.

He played a pivotal role in the controversy surrounding the birth of World Series Cricket in the late 1970s. Coming out of retirement in his early 40s, to again lead Australia, was an extraordinary contribution.

Bob Simpson became the first full-time coach of the Australian Cricket Team, in itself an innovation. His appointment was, I believe, a key ingredient in the great successes achieved by Australian cricketers, first under Allan Border's leadership when the Ashes were reclaimed in England in 1989 and the subsequent defeat by Mark Taylor's team of the West Indies in 1995.

As coach, Simpson practised a simple philosophy. In the following pages he describes it thus: 'The role of the coach is simple. To assist his charges to improve their skills and enhance their personal performance.' His aims are simple too. 'To create improvement so that a batsman scores more runs; a bowler takes more wickets; a fieldsman takes more catches, saves more runs in the field and seizes more opportunities to create run-outs ... '

Those words express succinctly the pragmatic, results-oriented approach which Bob Simpson brought to his very successful years as coach of the Australian Cricket Team.

They also reveal his single-minded application to the game which he applied when he was a member and later Captain of the Australian team.

Literally a mountain of cricket books have been written over the years. Few Australian giants of the game could possibly hope to match the different perspectives, the length of active participation at the top, nor the breadth of experience which Bob Simpson brings as author of this book.

I am sure that this book will bring pleasure to thousands of cricketing fans all around the world. It is a privilege to write this brief foreword.

JOHN HOWARD
August, 1996

Left: Bob Simpson (right) with David Boon during the tickertape parade that was held in Sydney to celebrate Australia's victory in the West Indies in 1995.

Prelude
by Steve Waugh

It was only hours after the finish of the third Test of Australia's 1995 series in the Caribbean. The West Indies had inflicted a crushing defeat upon us, at Port of Spain, in Trinidad, on a day which before play had promised so much but in the end delivered nothing but pain. The team was now gathered in room 522 of the Trinidad Hilton. It wasn't a crisis meeting; more a 'think-tank' on how to prepare for the upcoming and decisive fourth Test at Sabina Park, Kingston, Jamaica — for so long a graveyard ground for visiting teams.

It was at this meeting that Bob Simpson said something which, at the time, stirred up mixed emotions among the players, most notably myself. Simmo addressed the batsmen: 'You guys are not doing the job properly. No-one is taking it upon themselves to put their hand up and make a big score. Instead, you're getting starts and then throwing them away. It's been happening all tour.'

I couldn't let this comment go, as I believed we had all been short-changed by such a statement. I let Simmo know that, in my opinion, our lack of big scores wasn't due to a lack of application, but more to do with the quality of our opponents. Unfortunately, this was a point of view that Simmo couldn't bring himself to even partly acknowledge. In the end, we agreed to disagree.

It probably wasn't until some hours later that I started thinking again about this conversation. With the benefit of time, I came to the conclusion that Simmo's point was valid. In my case, I had been consistent all tour. But I was yet to post a big score befitting my good form . . . perhaps this was due to me not being quite committed to grinding things out and working through the tough periods. It was during these moments of brutal self-assessment that I vowed to be the one to 'put my hand up' and do the job if the opportunity arose.

The rest, I guess, is history. We became the first team in 15 years to break the Windies' phenomenal run at Test level, by winning the fourth Test by an innings. And I contributed a career-best 200. While the hard work in making this score had to be done by myself, it was certainly encouraged by the comments that had pricked my conscience a few days before the game. This was a perfect example of a coach doing his job without anyone outside of the team knowing about it, and also a perfect example of Bob Simpson the man. He has, on many occasions, offended players and media alike with his methods and comments, but the bottom line is: he always wanted Australia to win. If he thought you weren't doing everything in your power to reach that objective, you became a casualty. This, perhaps, explains why quite a few players had their international aspirations cut short in the so-called 'Simpson era'. If you asked Bob, though, he would make no apologies. He considered such a philosophy a necessity if Australia were to climb from the depths of the cellar, which is where the team was when he took over as coach late in the 1985–86 season, to the top of the international tree.

My first acquaintance with Bob Simpson was on a sunny spring Sunday morning back in 1984, when I turned up for my initial appearance as part of the NSW Sheffield Shield squad. I was extremely nervous, not only because I was among such revered company in the playing ranks, but also because I would be working under the tutelage of one of Australia's greats, Bob Simpson, who was then the NSW coach. However, I was immediately put at ease by some comforting words from Simmo. More importantly, he gave me confidence in my own ability, and in the years to come he never tried to stifle my natural tendencies or instincts.

Not long after, we were re-united when Bob became coach of the Australian team in the same season that I had been fortunate enough to be chosen, as a 20-year-old, to represent my country. As I remember those early tough years, a complete change of attitude had to take place among the team in order for it to be competitive at the top level. Simmo demanded such a change and introduced measures that were a shock to many and, as a result, some did perish in a harsh environment. Looking back, though, such a move was a necessity, for we were playing and training like amateurs. It all began with fielding sessions that went for hours and were focused on improving techniques, while at the same time being competitive and, consequently, fun to be a part of. In addition, we were all made aware of our responsibilities, on and off the field — but when you are being told these home truths by men like Allan Border and Bob Simpson, you don't have to be Einstein to know that what you are receiving is valuable advice.

Our progression as a team wasn't startling but, nevertheless, evident to those involved with the side. The real worth of our new approach finally showed itself when we lifted the Reliance World Cup in 1987, to the surprise of the worldwide cricketing fraternity.

With this victory our self-esteem and belief in ourselves grew to new levels and an emphatic series win was soon ours in England, to the tune of 4–0. By this time, other teams had well and truly sat up and taken notice, with many implementing our team fielding drills in an attempt to bring their standards up to ours. On this '89 tour we developed from being a good side, to one on the verge of being a great one. There was an atmosphere and spirit within the team that made us almost unbeatable. It was a unique tour in that everyone got on fabulously, the cricket was always enjoyable and every player received great satisfaction from each other's successes. We played positive, aggressive cricket on each and every day on tour, a plan that was to be the cornerstone to our success and a formula that we all enjoyed adhering to.

Soon after, though, my own international career took a nosedive and I found myself on the outer, and in dire need of a tough self-assessment. It wasn't until the season of '92–93 that I returned, complete with a new level of consistency. This turnaround was largely due to a lot of soul searching and hard work, and also to a comment Simmo had made to me during my rehabilitation. He informed me that he, like myself, had been troubled by the short ball from the faster bowlers during his career. His solution was simple: don't worry about how you look, only about surviving the best way you can. On top of this simple advice came a tip on a small technical deficiency that had, without me realising, crept into my game.

So after 10 years of hard work from both the players and the coach, and a little more than a week after that team meeting in Trinidad, we all sat and celebrated at Sabina Park, on top of the cricketing pecking order. This was a fine and just tribute to all those involved in our evolution into a top-quality cricket team.

If one were to judge a coach purely on statistics, it must be said that the reign of Bob Simpson as Australian coach was supreme. In doing it his way, though, he will always have detractors. I believe that, as a coach, if you are doing your job correctly, you can't possibly be liked by everyone. You must make the difficult calls to get your team to where you want them to get to. Not everyone is going to agree with your methods, tactics or theories, but you owe it to yourself to stick to your beliefs. I believe Simmo has always done that. He has left Australian cricket in a healthier state than when he took over and has implemented a new professionalism that will be the benchmark for future Australian cricket sides to emulate.

For that we should all be grateful.

Introduction

Everybody wants a simple answer, a simple philosophy, something they can write on a dressing-room wall which will inspire them and ensure that they win matches. Coaches are supposed to have all the answers. While there is more to the game from a coach's point of view than simplistic slogans, there are basic principles that should not be lost in a welter of theories and philosophies.

In my opinion, the role of the cricket coach is simple: to assist cricketers in improving their skills and enhancing their personal performance. The coach's aims should be simple, too. A coach must create improvement, so that a batsman scores more runs, a bowler takes more wickets and a fieldsman takes more catches, saves more runs in the field and seizes more opportunities to create run-outs.

What does a cricket coach need to achieve these aims? Obviously he or she must possess knowledge of all aspects of the sport, plus the ability to communicate effectively with cricketers. Plus enthusiasm. Plus a love and passion for the game and the desire to instil these attributes in those seeking support and guidance.

As I write this book, I have been involved in cricket at the first-class level for some 43 years and I still have the same fascination for the game today that I had as a teenager. I still get an enormous kick out of being involved and contributing to the development of cricket. I love being a hands-on coach and getting out in the middle with the guys. Watching cricket is a joy and I seldom miss a ball. Neither should I, because a good coach should be able to recall virtually all the incidents in a day's play so attention can be drawn to them and the players' questions can be answered with authority. You cannot do that if you do not concentrate on the game. By the way, I have been guilty of sleeping at my post only once, when I dozed off in the dressing room at Gwalior in India after a particularly heavy night. But more of that later.

Enthusiasm is undoubtedly one of the main assets of a good coach. In fact, he or she has to be the most enthusiastic member of the team because it is the coach's responsibility to communicate that enthusiasm and maintain the keenness of the players at all times.

I judge a practice session where I am the coach in two ways. Is it noisy and bubbly? Are the players enjoying it? If the answer to either question is no, then I am not doing my job and I have to put it right. Recognising and solving problems is another basic but vital requirement of a good coach. I am not just talking about technical or purely cricket matters here. Often outside influences play a major role in the quality of an individual's or team's performance and every effort must be made to identify such influences and solve any problems they may cause.

Technical cricket worries are a quite different matter. No player's worries should be overlooked or treated lightly, whether they are considered real or imaginary. If a player feels there is a problem, it is a threat to that player's ability to perform properly. All cricketers at one time or another will be beset by uncertainties. In their mind the problems are real, irrespective of whether their coach or other players see it that way.

Inevitably, this is a very testing situation for a coach, who initially should go through a mental checklist to see if the player really does have a technical problem. If this process draws a blank, the coach continues the search by trying to discover if there is a problem outside of cricket which is affecting that player's performance. If nothing shows up, then the 'white tablet' cure may be called for. By this I mean the coach might have to invent a problem. And then solve it.

In such circumstances, the coach makes it very obvious to the player that he or she is being singled out for special scrutiny. The player is watched from all angles, after being told that the coach is working very hard on this mysterious problem. A bit of play-acting does not go amiss — perhaps a long discussion with the bowlers in the nets if the player with the problem is a batsman, followed by a near-theatrical walk down into the net. You call the batsman over and apologise for being so slow. 'Sorry,' you might say, 'I should have spotted it ages ago.'

The 'solution' should be kept basic. 'Your head is not steady,' is always good advice, as is, 'Your initial movement is not sharp enough.' So, too, is the suggestion that 'you are picking the bat up too late.' If the troubled player is a bowler, the magical remedy should be just as simple. The run-up is always good for a cure. 'You are pushing too early,' is a logical remedy. Or perhaps: 'Your head is not steady.' Or: 'You are not accelerating through the crease.'

Invariably the players are delighted, because a weight has been lifted from their shoulders. They can concentrate on a point which is, in any case, fundamental to their game while really believing that they have overcome a flaw.

And why is this approach called the 'white tablet' treatment. Some years ago, Australia were playing Pakistan and the Pakistani batsmen suffered a whole series of misadventures. However, fortunately, the Australian physiotherapist-cum-doctor-cum-psychiatric nurse, Errol Alcott, had a magic cure: 'You keep your own players so fit. How do you do it?' he had been asked by the Pakistan management, after yet another of the visitors had collapsed in pain. Errol produced a white tablet and handed it over with a wink. Within five minutes, the stricken Pakistani was back on his feet, sound in wind and limb, in what for all the world seemed to be a miracle of modern medicine!

Errol still keeps a few white Smarties in his medical kit. Just in case...

For any cricket coach, and teacher really, just as important as being able to solve problems, real and imaginary, is being able to explain why they occur. I am very much a 'Why' coach, in that my usual approach to emphasising a point is something like, 'I believe if you try it this way your game will benefit for these reasons.'

While cricket has always been a game of theories, I do believe that we are currently exploring more theories than ever. The increasing availability of technology to help coaches has led to more thoughts and ideas being bandied

about than ever before. There is nothing wrong with that, but we should be able to apply the 'Why' principle before we grasp hold of new ideas as gospel. Simply being new does not make an idea correct any more than it makes it wrong.

A coach guiding the minds, ambitions and futures of young players must be as certain as possible that what is being preached is sound. I suppose it is every coach's dream to come up with an idea or method which will produce instant champions. And we only have to look at the profusion of books, videos and tapes on golf to see that cricket is not the only game with a thousand theories. Some are useful; many are no more than marketing exercises. Watch the most successful golfers, the real tournament pros, and you see orthodoxy. Individual styles, of course, but orthodox swings suggesting that the basics have not changed over many years. Or look at the classically-styled clubs all the top players use. The best players are sticking very closely to the fundamentals of their sport.

The coach has a heavy responsibility — the opportunity to help or hinder the players who require support. The coach's job is to make them better players, better team people, better sports persons, even better citizens. Be sure when you accept the responsibility that you have the unselfishness that has to go with it.

We are all ambitious and like recognition. That is natural enough, but if you get into cricket coaching purely from those motives you have missed the point. The greatest satisfaction and reward has to come from watching the pleasure players get from the improvement the coach's input has helped create. It is only then that the coach's ambition and responsibility has been fulfilled. All people in cricket are trustees of a great game. Let's leave it better for our involvement in it.

And what about sleeping in the dressing room? I own up. During the Australian team's 1986 tour of India we played a match in Gwalior, where the Maharaja was very much a cricket person and very proud of his city and its history. Madhavrao Scindia was then Minister for Railways in Rajiv Gandhi's government and later president of the 1987 World Cup organising committee. He staged an outstanding barbecue dinner for both teams and an evening later invited Allan Border, tour manager Alan Crompton and me for dinner at his palace. To cut a long story short we arrived early, sat down late and were desperately trying to take our leave in the early hours of the morning when the Maharaja organised a sightseeing tour of the city by horse and carriage. AB took the reins, which probably said something for the state we were all in. I hate to think what time it was before we got back to our hotel, but I confess to sleeping in the dressing room on the last day while AB sweated it out on the playing field.

CHAPTER 1

Keith Stackpole played 43 Test matches with a hell of a lot of distinction and is a thoughtful and articulate commentator on the game — but he still recalls the first time he tried to air his knowledge in the Test arena. It was the fifth Test against England, Melbourne, 1966. 'Stackie' was probably feeling a bit worldly in front of his home crowd, especially since Australia had won the previous Test by an innings. The England opener, Bob Barber, was playing and missing regularly, as he usually did, when Stackie walked up to me and wicketkeeper Wally Grout and observed: 'Gee, this bloke can't play at all, can he?'

Wally glared at his young team-mate, who had one whole Test match behind him, and said icily: 'When you've played 12 or 15 Tests, Stackie, you can venture an opinion about other players. While you're still playing your second just stand there quietly, watch and learn why players become successful.' Stackie, suitably chastened, beat a hasty retreat.

The fact that Keith remembers the incident to this day without a hint of injustice confirms the value of the right sort of peer influence and education. Wally Grout's retort was not intended to be cruel; it did assert strongly that there was a right way and a wrong way to approach the game.

If you are smart, you never stop learning. I know I learned as much about cricket after I retired as I did when I played it for a living. I had a good knowledge when I retired, but then I went on radio and television and had to relate to others just what was going on. It wasn't easy to take the new perspective; some very good players are never able to explain to others what they themselves did intuitively. No doubt the modern players will come across a black-and-white video of Bob Simpson batting and discover whether what he advised them to do and what he did himself were the same thing. It's a bit of a worry. I can promise them that I've looked at old videos of myself and I reckon I practised what I preach. More or less... I was never a major critic of World Series Cricket, even though back in 1977–78 I led the official Australian side in opposition to it and was as aware as anyone of the strong passions which it aroused at that time. WSC was a fact of life and eventually of history; and has had a lasting effect on cricket in Australia, even worldwide. And it is perfectly arguable that some of its legacies have been beneficial to the game as a whole. However, in one respect it was a distinctly bad influence, because it disturbed the tradition in Australian cricket of peer influence which had grown up over many years and which was the basis of player education at the top level, from one generation to the next.

As a player who had grown up in an atmosphere where players were ready to help each other and where senior players regarded it as one of their responsibilities, I soon noticed the difference in attitudes created by World Series Cricket.

Players became more protective of their positions and less likely to pass on advice and experience; even in the nets, the feeling that senior players were there to help less seasoned ones disappeared. The WSC split created divisions which were easily seen and, less obvious but just as threatening, created a more selfish attitude in the game. It was obviously going to take time to repair, long after the negotiators at boardroom level had shaken hands and announced that everything was back to normal...

The tradition of handing down experience from one generation to the next was fundamental to the cricket roots I grew up in and no doubt for ages before that. It involved rough as well as smooth, the willingness of older players to bring the young upstart down a peg or two, but it was generally a benign sort of education process. Young players who are good enough to make the grade to high-quality teams really do feel they know everything; the brashness of youth and all that. It sometimes comes as quite a shock when they realise how little they know.

In September 1987 I was asked to prepare a paper on the state of Australian cricket. At the time, the Australian team was at a relatively low ebb. Two years before, some of its best players had accepted lucrative offers to go on a 'rebel' tour of South Africa. An Ashes series in Australia had just been lost. What I wrote sounds pretty gloomy now, but it reflected the malaise of the game and the need to do something about it at the time.

This is what I wrote:

Australian cricket has probably gone through more changes and turmoil in the last 10 years than in any other decade in the history of the game.

Inevitably, the major ones to suffer in conflicts are the direct combatants, in this case, the players.

While the crises created through WSC and the South African defections may have assisted the players to receive greater payments, infighting and selfishness have destroyed some of the great strengths of Australian cricket. This is particularly seen in the diminishing role of the Australian captain within the team and the almost total destruction of peer influence within Australian cricket.

The Australian cricket captain always had a rather unique and envied position in Australian sport. Whilst obviously answerable to the Australian Cricket Board, he held an almost autonomous position. For instance, when on tour he was the centre pin around which the tour revolved. He generally handled the Press, spoke first at functions, and if only one speech was to be made, he delivered it. With the help of his senior players, he supervised practice and assisted in developing the skills of players in the team. He also became something of a father confessor to his charges.

This system worked wonderfully well, for the players responded to the fact that a fellow player, not an official, was in charge and generally a very close relationship was allowed to develop within the team. In addition, I believe a far greater team involvement was possible under this system, with various members being given responsibility to handle physical training, fielding sessions and so on. Instead of just being a team member, they became an important cog in the side and generally responded to the extra responsibility.

Traditionally, the senior members of the side took over the coaching of newcomers. It generally was not on an organised or even a delegated basis — it was just something they accepted as their role and responsibility to the team. There was never a big thing made of peer influence and, in fact, it was not until I looked back on my career when I was captain that I even realised the pattern had developed.

Unfortunately, due to many circumstances, peer influence has virtually disappeared, much to the detriment of Australian cricket. Perhaps the saddest aspect is that not only has it nearly gone at top level, but also in the grade and district ranks. Whereas most district teams had a couple of old hard heads who ran the team, kept the youngsters on the straight and narrow and coached them as well, these days very few of those senior players are left. As a result, the youngsters have to make their way on their own.

At the top level, it is probably easier to explain why things have changed, with so much turmoil over the last decade or so and players often appearing to be preoccupied with sorting out off-field matters such as contracts and the like. At the lower level there is no easy explanation, except perhaps that these days no-one seems to have the time, or wants to make the time, to put something back into cricket.

Whatever the reason, there is no doubt in my mind that the decline in peer influence has played perhaps the major role in the decline of Australian cricket. I say this having been so closely involved in Australian cricket for such a long period and particularly over the last decade. The players of today are still being blessed with the same amount of natural skill as in any previous era, but, unfortunately, we are not turning this skill into winning performances.

Obviously, the decline in peer influence is not the only reason for disappointing performances in recent years. Unfortunately, in this same decade there has been a sad withdrawal from teaching the skills and fundamentals of cricket and a concentration on what I consider lesser needs, an overemphasis on physical fitness, diet, motivation and so on.

No-one believes in physical fitness more than I do. However, when fitness is presented as a cure-all and a way to instant success, and is not allied to skills, then I am concerned. Over the last 10 to 15 years, too much emphasis has been placed on physical training and valuable time has been wasted by well-intentioned but unfortunately ill-advised coaches and administrators who believed that extra fitness was a sure-fire, magical way of ensuring success. Undoubtedly this has affected our cricket, with the development of skills and techniques almost neglected in the quest for greater physical strength.

It is interesting that modern coaching methods, diet, a more scientific approach to training and all the rest has not been able to prevent work-related injuries on the sports field. Modern bowlers, for instance, seem to break down more often than their predecessors. I don't think that it is just a matter of extra publicity or awareness of injuries; I think today's bowlers really are more vulnerable than bowlers used to be. I also believe that lifestyle has an awful lot to do with that. There is a theory that past generations were better set up physically because they used both sides of the brain more than we do now — and that brain-use was related to their lifestyle. Sounds complicated, I know, but the bottom line seems to be that the kids of a previous and more physically-demanding generation developed a natural fitness which now has to be acquired.

I really believe that a lot of cricketers have injury problems — and often from an early age — because of the easy lifestyle we all enjoy. When I was a kid I walked everywhere, climbed trees and jumped fences for fun. I did a lot of physical work without ever thinking it had anything to do with fitness and conditioning. Yet, I'm sure it did. When I see modern players suffering from back troubles, shin soreness, stress fractures and the like, I can't believe that they are caused simply by the physical demands of sport. Rather, I don't believe kids get the physical conditioning they developed quite naturally years ago. They also don't play as many sports as previous generations used to so their bodies are not trained, in the widest sense, for physical exertion.

Around the time I broke into the NSW state team, my normal weekend activities in the winter consisted of golf on Saturday morning, soccer in the afternoon, tennis Sunday morning and baseball in the afternoon. And I always went to the dance on Saturday night.

So, I covered a lot of sports, used a lot of muscles and energy, and in the process developed the physical condition that was encouraged by lifestyle rather than compromised by easy living. We went through a period where it became fashionable to encourage kids to specialise rather than to enjoy a variety of sports and I think that didn't help their general physical development. Strain-type injuries in cricket are becoming quite a problem and I'm sure the good life has a lot to do with it.

I believe it should be mainly the player's responsibility to get himself fit in his own time so that the limited time available for group training can be utilised to develop the essential skills and techniques needed to meet the demands of cricket at its highest level. Unfortunately, over the last decade or so, many teams have been in the hands of people whose skills lie in physical training. Naturally, they have concentrated on areas they are comfortable with rather than the more demanding development and improvement of cricketing skills. While physical fitness, diet and motivation are important, they should not be the dominant factors in the development of skills and should not be seen as instant ways of ensuring success.

Australian cricket at all levels has more designated coaches now than at any time in the history of the game. Yet, there has never been another period in my experience where the players so urgently need coaching. This is clearly shown by the amount of time I spend with the Australian team making simple but necessary corrections to their techniques. Even such fundamentals as turning blind and going down to field the ball on the wrong knee are commonplace. Such obvious basics should have been spotted and attended to at school level or grade ranks at worst! That players have been allowed to carry basic faults to Test level is a sad indictment of our system and must be remedied urgently.

While we have an excellent scheme in place to encourage coaches to improve their skills, it would appear there is a blind spot which allows players to progress with obvious flaws. I have little doubt that all coaches who had some input into players reaching Test level would know the right and wrong way to execute the manoeuvres I have mentioned, but nothing has been done to educate the players. Picking up and correcting mistakes is just about the major part of coaching. It is not that difficult to do and I believe that all our training manuals and training classes for coaches should include a segment on the subject. It is not much good having an extensive coaching system if the coaches are not capable of remedying simple fundamental faults.

While it has been suggested that the youngsters of today do not take kindly to advice, my experience has shown that they thirst for knowledge and it is up to us to provide this knowledge so that they can utilise the natural skills they have.

That report was written almost a decade ago and there is no doubt that we have come a long way towards re-establishing a healthy hierarchy in the Test squad since then. It didn't just happen; it took a lot of effort, planning and co-operation on the part of many people involved to reach a stage where Australian cricket has rediscovered a great deal of its identity. The successes that Australia has enjoyed in recent years have been all the sweeter because they were achieved from a very unsound base.

It is popular practice to talk about international players as 'naturally gifted' and to regard the Australian set-up as laden with talented individuals who would have made it through without anybody's help.

There is a lot of talent about, no doubt about that, but that talent has to be carefully nurtured and developed to deal with modern pressures and demands. I am not suggesting the pressures of today are unique but they are different from those faced a generation ago. More than ever, players need the shared experience of others if they are to make the difficult transition into the top-flight game.

I was fortunate, like most of my generation, because I had the example and advice of a lot of senior players right from the start of my cricketing career. Whether I was a kid playing for Petersham-Marrickville in Sydney grade, an ambitious young bloke making his way in the Sheffield Shield, or a nervous tyro in Test cricket, there was always an old hand and an old head ready to show me the ropes. It wasn't always a pat on the back or the reassurance that I was the best thing since sliced bread either. Good advice is usually what you need to hear rather than what you want to hear.

COACHING IS ALL ABOUT WHY. Unfortunately, it is often approached as an exercise in how: how to best play a certain stroke, how to stand, how to achieve a level of technical excellence so that somebody from the MCC coaching manual can come along and take a snap. And, above all, how to look good.

Kids taking an interest in the game at an early age don't need that kind of tuition and react badly, no wonder, to hours of mechanical, boring drills. More mature cricketers wanting to improve their game invariably respond to an outline of why they are making mistakes and why certain adjustments will make them more effective players. I remember an old Chinese proverb along the lines of: 'Give a man a fish and you feed him for a day. Teach him to fish and you feed him for life.' Cricket coaching is a bit like that. A player who knows why some things work better than others is going to be more effective than the bloke who just copies the style.

Modern education in schools leans towards the belief that kids should be inquisitive and questioning, that they should find things out and work things out for themselves. This means youngsters are no longer inclined to accept a set of rules without understanding the philosophy behind them. The budding cricketer is entitled to know why some approaches work better than others. Telling them to 'keep your left elbow up and play straight' simply isn't enough. When a seasoned player is going through a bad spell he always wants to know why; discovering what he is doing wrong is the first step to putting it right. The philosophy of coaching is simple enough: to make a player a better player, for himself and for the team.

That's why I firmly believe that coaching has a place at every level of the game. There is a much-publicised theory that the very best players, those of international standard, have outgrown their need for coaching. The suggestion is that coaching will somehow detract from the naturalness of their game and be counter productive. I regard that as a load of baloney and so, it seems, do most of the world's most successful sports people. Golfers and tennis stars make millions from their skills and they are never far from their coaches — not because they need instruction in how to hold a club or racket but because they constantly encounter new problems and are professional enough to look for advice. They constantly want to know why. The world's best golfers play a round with the help of a caddie who is clearly not as good a player as they are; but his advice is invaluable because he knows their game and has an eye for detail. No matter what his game, the more a player learns about himself the more effective he is likely to be. The ones who think they can stop learning come to grief and it is rubbish to pretend that international players have passed beyond the need for coaching and advice.

In the mid 1990s, we in Australia have a plague of batsmen who are pointing their front foot in the wrong direction. A very basic fault has become a fashion — partly, I think, because of the influence of the Ian Chappell era. Ian's 'back and across' method worked for him and was copied by players who weren't nearly as good as he was and whose natural style did not suit that approach. Ian could play all the way forward but a lot of his disciples cannot. So we have reached a period where too many batsmen are straddling the crease — when you do that, your foot automatically points towards point. From that position it is impossible to play the ball with the full face of the bat. Quite simply, the feet get in the way and strokes are played with only half a bat. It is possible to play away from the body, leaving a big gap, but much harder to get close in. That is why most defensive shots these days are played in the area between cover and third man. It is the sort of fault which can creep into any player's game, even the most experienced players.

In such a situation, the coach's first duty is to identify the problem, then do a lot of work to fix it. In my opinion, the real key — the thing that will eventually lead to the problem being eradicated — is determining the reasons why players are not using the full face of the bat. From that point, the 'cure' will be much less painful.

When I first went to Petersham-Marrickville, not long after the amalgamation of two proud and accomplished clubs, I rather fancied myself as a bit of a gun. I'd broken records at Under–16 level, made a few people sit up and take notice, and I reckoned I was ready for bigger things. Second grade, probably, just to begin with. I practised for a month with the blokes trying out for the four grade teams and nothing I saw changed my view that I was better than the players around me. A hint of cockiness, you might say. So when the teams were finally announced I naturally looked straight at the second-grade list. No R. Simpson. An oversight, obviously, must be in the thirds. No luck. And no R. Simpson in the fourth-grade team either. A bit rough, this cricket selection.

Right at the bottom of the team sheet was a list of about six players who would be allowed to train on... with R. Simpson's name last on the list! Talk about deflating. However, the choice was to stick with it or go back into the local junior association. A few matches later I was given a go in the fourths, then the thirds and after three matches there I was promoted to first grade. Less than 12 months after that I played for NSW.

While I was in the thirds the captain — he looked as old as Methuselah to me but he was probably about 35 — gave me what amounted to a pep talk. 'Don't expect to get the runs up here that you've been getting in the fourth grade,' he said helpfully. 'You won't get 100 or anything like that . . .' Considering he had me pencilled in at number seven in the batting order, that seemed a pretty safe prediction. We had a collapse, I went in relatively early and had made 98... when the captain closed our innings! So he was right about the century after all. Okay, so that may not be the best way to handle every young man with ambition and a belief in his ability, but there were some pretty tough characters about at every level of the game and their attitude was that everything had to be earned and learned. Anything which came easily or cheap was suspect. By deciding to fight my way from the bottom and not taking the attitude that the first setback was too much, I probably passed some sort of test. From then on, nobody in the club could do too much for me. The same sort of attitude was present in the NSW team.

Imagine walking into a dressing room which included champions such as Arthur Morris, Ray Lindwall, Keith Miller, Alan Davidson and Richie Benaud. And as a 16 year old with only a dozen first-grade matches at that! It was totally awe-inspiring. Arthur Morris turned me round, looked me up and down and demanded: 'Where are they, then?' Gulp. 'Where are what, Mr Morris?' 'Your bloody nappies. You're young enough . . .'

Arthur was absolutely marvellous; the whole team of legends were. I appreciated their help at the time, the way they would take me quietly on one side and talk about what it takes to be a real cricketer, but I didn't fully understand what they were doing. Helping to educate a younger team-mate was perfectly natural to them; peer influence was taken for granted. Years later, there was a huge vacuum when it temporarily went out of the game.

Young players, however talented, need the accumulated wisdom of others, the help of blokes who have been through the mill. Establishing a career as an international batsman, for instance, isn't just about having all the ability in the world; it's about being able to succeed consistently under all conditions. This is something that can only come from listening to experience and gaining experience. That is why I have always estimated the value of a Test player and a Test captain not just in terms of personal ability or matches won and lost, but also in terms of how many players they left behind in the game better off for their influence.

A captain may lead the most talented side in the world so his win-loss ratio should not be the only yardstick to his contribution to the game. Clive Lloyd had a tremendous run of success as captain of the West Indies but his teams were so strong that he only had to toss the ball in the air and rely on whoever caught it to bowl his sides to victory.

Passing on tips and experience is part of the traditions of the game. Established players regarded it as one of their responsibilities — but that attitude definitely waned during and immediately after the years of World Series Cricket. There was a much more selfish attitude around after WSC, an 'us and them' attitude where players were reluctant to help those outside their circle. It is often suggested that money warped the players' attitudes towards the game but I am not sure it is as simple as that.

What money undoubtedly has done is to make it attractive for players to extend their careers beyond an age where they might once have retired — and that means selectors will be seen to be more ruthless in dropping players who would once have walked away.

The threat to long traditions of peer influence in Australian cricket was very real in the mid 1980s and certainly worked alongside a number of other factors in reducing Australia's effectiveness in world cricket. Fortunately, we have regained a lot of ground and I take great pride in the fact that in the years since I compiled that report to the Australian Cricket Board I have had an input into the careers of many outstanding players.

I think my contribution has been positive and constructive, but I wonder, when you look at the contribution of some people in the game, whether they can say the same thing.

CHAPTER 2

The Australian way

When I first took over as Australia's coach in 1986, there were 44 players running around in the Sheffield Shield who had played in some form of international cricket. A joke. There has never been a period in history when Australia had 44 players good enough to play for their country. It was obvious the old shotgun selection method had been applied by someone desperately seeking a bit of success. However, this approach had not worked in the short term and the state of Australian cricket, after a 'rebel' tour to South Africa and the disastrous 1985 Ashes tour, demanded that some long-term planning and philosophy were urgently needed. Put simply, the national side was in a mess.

There were still talented players around, but it was obvious that many of them did not have the work ethic it would take to put Australian cricket back on its feet. As well, virtually nothing had been done to create a framework in which players could be groomed to fit into a Test side which had the right philosophies already in place. Every time a batsman scored a century or a bowler took a few wickets in the Shield, he was catapulted into the Australian team, fingers crossed. This had to change.

In my two seasons as coach of NSW (1984–86), I'd had an insight into the prevailing attitudes. Because the Blues team had achieved some success, I was asked to go on the 1986 Australian tour to New Zealand, to assess the team situation and see how I felt about coaching the national side. To be perfectly frank, I was pretty horrified by what I saw.

In many cases, the work ethic was non-existent. In fact, I had to reduce the intensity of my usual training routines by up to half because, although the NSW boys were used to it, so many of the other players could not keep up. What was worse, they did not seem to want to match up. Instead, they treated the whole training exercise as a bit of a joke, in order, I believe, to disguise the fact that they couldn't hack it. Taken out of their comfort zone, they fell back on schoolboy humour and the pretence that it all didn't really matter. Back in Australia, I made my feelings known to the Board and they responded by inviting me to become coach and, subsequently, a selector.

I must admit I was a bit reluctant to take on the selector's role at first, because I did not know if it would compromise my coaching. However, having coached the side for a while without really knowing what the selectors were aiming for, I decided that it was important at this point for me to take on this dual role. From that time on, I believe we worked with a purpose and with a real goal in mind — not simply where Australian cricket needed to be tomorrow, but where it should be a couple of years down the track and beyond.

I was fortunate because the other selectors of the time — chairman Lawrie Sawle, Jim Higgs and Greg Chappell — were just as anxious to look to the future and develop a philosophy to achieve long-term ends. We decided what style of player we would need and agreed to try to work with a flexible group of around 16 and give them every opportunity to prove themselves. After a relatively short time it became obvious that some were not going to make it and would have to be replaced; others such as David Boon, Geoff Marsh and Steve Waugh were going to be very good players in the long term if we were prepared to back them.

There are no magic wands in selecting a team or a squad and there were bound to be contentious selections and omissions. Everybody has a theory and a favourite. However, nobody was dismissed out of hand and nobody was automatically rejected, however convenient their excuse afterwards, because they had picked up the wrong knife at dinner or tied the wrong knot in their tie. Sadly, there were real natural talents who had not been properly schooled in their early days and consequently would never fulfil their potential. David Hookes was one of the best examples of that. A very gifted batsman who had been regarded as a real catch for World Series Cricket back in the late '70s, Hookes became a superstar before he was a star or even a genuinely established international player. Hookes was used by WSC to provide glamour and living proof that all the best young players were flocking to the rebel cause. Unfortunately, at that time in his career I believe his publicity outstripped his ability as a batsman, and because of this he lost the opportunity to fully develop his undoubted natural ability.

As selectors, we pondered long and hard on what we had and where we wanted to go. What should be the right balance and make-up of the side? How would we create a team which would win matches playing the Australian way? And was there even an Australian way to be exploited?

Although the overall approach of the Australian cricket team might have varied from decade to decade, the basic virtues of being mentally aggressive, busy, positive and energetic had always done Australia proud in the past. So we asked the players to re-create these qualities. We felt we had a solid base, something we could work on, in the opening partnership of Marsh and Boon. Allan Border would always be averaging at least 50 in middle-order, while Steve Waugh, then only 21 but highly promising, batted at six (ironically, it was his bowling which often kept him in the side back in those days). Another young batsman, Dean Jones, was learning his trade fast and becoming a much more rounded player, as he showed with a fabulous double century in the tied Test match in Madras in late 1986. Tim Zoehrer had all the makings of an excellent wicketkeeper who could bat effectively at the top-level. In the bowling department, we had Craig McDermott, who as a teenager had enjoyed a highly encouraging start to his international career but then lost his way, and Bruce Reid, a man with the potential to be one of the all-time greats. Greg Matthews was bowling off spin well. And there were others with the ability to develop, including Simon Davis and Simon O'Donnell, while batsmen like Greg Ritchie and Wayne Phillips appeared to be men who would be asked to provide more than it appeared they were prepared to give.

What we did — and this is where the other selectors were excellent in terms of interaction with the selector-coach — was say to the players: 'This is the way we think we can play best if we are going to make an impact in the future. We will stick with you as long as we can, provided you back this philosophy.' At least we knew where we wanted to go.

It was a bit of a jigsaw in the early days, trying to fit the pieces together and create a big picture. A really good team performance was almost a bonus early on; we took what consolation we could from the better days and tried to learn from everything that went right or wrong. Boon was pencilled in as having the potential to be a cornerstone of the side. However, we lost him for a while, when he struggled against England in Australia in 1986–87, which simply shows that individual form cannot be dictated by a team plan, however enthusiastically drawn. But, of course, David came back so strongly after that. In fact, AB was really the only one you could rely on consistently and that put a lot of strain on him at the time. It was hard to expect him to enjoy his cricket when he always felt he was the first piece in a domino theory.

What we did do was develop enthusiasm in the side, which became the priceless asset behind everything we subsequently achieved. No group of cricketers has ever worked harder than the World Cup-winning squad in 1987; they accepted an amazing workload with an enthusiasm which left other teams open-mouthed and they really enjoyed their own improvement. For me, that was the breakthrough we needed to show that our philosophies were right and that the system we had put in place was effective.

Lawrie Sawle has to take a lot of the credit for that, a superb chairman of selectors with a skill for encouraging everyone to have a point of view without losing sight of the objectives. The discussion was often hard and forthright, but never acrimonious. In fact, I do not recall us ever taking a vote on this player or that. Lawrie encouraged discussion right down to the wire and then individual members of the selection panel would concede to the majority view. You do that more readily when you know everybody really is working towards the same end and there was a very tangible sense of common purpose. Even though we were a pretty diverse lot as people, opinionated, of course, and with attitudes developed by years of our own experience, we were all trying to head in the same direction.

Greg Chappell was always a solid influence. I think he found it hard to come to terms with the fact that not all players are as good as he was and that made him very demanding, but he was not intolerant and accepted the realities of what we had. When Greg resigned, one of his former Australian team-mates John Benaud — super-aggressive and always a bit over the top — moved in. First ball had to be hit back over the bowler's head, off-spinners can't bowl, every leg-spinner is a gem who must be polished and preserved, were some of John's opinions... a bit tongue in cheek, one of the attitudes you need around any selection table. John was very conscientious, very positive in his attitudes and a great lover of the game of cricket who, incidentally, had returned when he was over 40 to captain his club's fifth-grade team... on the understanding that he could have three spinners in the side.

Jim Higgs, himself a former Test leggie, was always the wild card, a stirrer who would throw in a new idea just when you thought the issue was settled and insist on worrying it to death. I'm sure that sometimes he was just winding us up, but it certainly led to some animated discussion.

Several of our selection meetings were held via telephone link-ups, which could have been an absolute shambles except that our basic philosophies were the same and we already knew how each of us felt about individuals and the team plan. Still, our discussion could go on for anything up to three hours — depending how inventive Jim was — and every line was open so you could hear the sighs and groans and chuckles of the others as you climbed aboard your hobby horse. Every selector has his preferences, his favourites if you like. The trick is not to let personalities warp your judgment and the other selectors usually see to that.

One thing we determined at the outset was to give everyone a chance, to back our judgment and not to react to outside pressures, wherever they may come from. Sometimes it is necessary to take a punt, as in the case of Ian Healy, who learned so much of his cricket actually playing internationally. When Ian was first selected, Greg Chappell was the only one who had seen him play and he really went in to bat for him, which was a superb assessment.

Okay, so Ian, like Greg, is a Queenslander, but parochialism was one factor which never came into our discussions. Nobody pushed his state just because he was a Victorian, a Queenslander or whatever. So many state officials push their own world-beaters hard and bemoan the fact that they have not got enough representatives in the national side. I admire their enthusiasm. It is impossible to come away from any state without a comprehensive list of local world-beaters waiting to take international cricket by storm. It is no part of an Australian selector's job, however, to push parochial interests. Some years ago I was flying into Perth with Lawrie Sawle, who, most unlike him, admitted that he wasn't looking forward to going home. 'I have just realised that there isn't a Western Australian in the Test side,' he said. 'Can you imagine the flack I'll take for that?' The point, entirely to his credit, was that he had not noticed until after the team had been picked.

We felt as selectors that we had identified basic problems and we were looking forward, probably further than most selection panels in the past. Knowing that fashions change, we always tried to keep an open mind and avoid the obvious. Understandably enough, ever since Dennis Lillee had retired there had been a popular clamour to find his successor. However, Lillees do not grow on trees and we realised that if we became obsessed with the search for the great fast bowler of the age we might miss a genuine swing bowler — and nobody who had seen Alan Davidson's era doubted what another Davo could do for Australian cricket.

ATTITUDES IN CRICKET WILL ALWAYS CHANGE BECAUSE CRICKET IS PART OF A CHANGING SOCIETY. It is bound to be influenced by social and economic forces, by the desire to improve itself or even by the desire to resist change for its own sake.

I was asked not long ago to produce a paper entitled 'Cricket the Australian Way' and that wasn't as easy or straightforward as some might think. A particularly Australian way of cricket probably existed before World War II, when we did not tour very often and were not as exposed as we are now to overseas players and attitudes. The pre-War game was settled and sure of itself, played on the best batting wickets the game has ever seen. It was the 'Golden Age' of cricket according to some, although I doubt if bowlers were quite as enthused. The flat, predictable nature of the pitches meant that rawboned pace and perseverance weren't enough in themselves to dislodge good batsmen, so bowlers had to develop guile and skill. The odd out-and-out fast bowler came along, but there was no concerted search for killer pace; swing bowlers and spinners were highly prized and the game owed much of its character to them. Batsmen were basically back-foot players, most of them hooked, and were strong cutters and on-side players. And they were aggressive in the field, one trait at least which has always been characteristically Australian. This was the 'Australian Way' in a nutshell. However, a heck of a lot of changes have occurred since the War, some in terms of attitude and some in terms of how we followed the latest fads and fashions.

That said, on a broad level, I think the structure of cricket in Australia today is very nearly ideal — light years ahead of the rest of the world in most respects. There are concerns about the volume of cricket being played in schools and that is a problem being faced internationally, but I think Australia was quicker than most to recognise the dangers and do something about them. Structured school cricket is only part of the system now; so many matches are played outside school hours and parents are encouraged to take a very active part in the organisation of matches and associations. There is a huge parent input and that is vital to the future. The networking is very strong, so that if a youngster shows real ability by the time he is 15 or 16, the cricket grapevine will have taken notice of him.

All the state associations these days have country-based coaches as well as close-monitoring of the city scene, so there is constant feedback and information flowing both ways. Very few players escape the net. The path for young players is clearly marked from their local associations through to representative honours at several age levels. By the time they reach an age where they might be selected for the Australian Cricket Academy — and the public discovers them — they are already known performers and have a magnificent grounding in the game. I don't think any other nation has such a comprehensive system. To make this system work takes a lot of time and effort, of course, and from a large amount of people who don't get a lot of credit for what they put in. The grass-roots strength of Australian cricket is also its strength at the top; so long as we keep that in mind the game will be in good hands.

However, the game cannot stand still and I know from experience how attitudes and expectations change from generation to generation. The changes are quicker now; I was out of top cricket for 10 years after I first retired in 1968 and although I played club cricket and thought I was in touch, I was struck by the changes in thinking at international level when I returned to the Australian side during the WSC years. The speed of change is so great that I don't think anyone who had been out of the picture for 10 years could come back and fit in these days. 〉

By 1988, the jigsaw was falling into place. One of the things we were on the lookout for was a left-handed opening batsman. We really felt that the combination of right-handed and left-handed opener was a huge tactical benefit to a Test side, and, fortunately, along came a player whose technique might not yet have been the world's greatest but who did have a wonderful temperament that was built on the ability to totally ignore the previous delivery. Here was a bloke who shrugged off the fact that he had just played and missed three times and got on with the job. His arrival meant that David Boon could move to number three, always a potential problem position, and we had extra flexibility down the order.

Welcome Mark Taylor.

The team which evolved and which re-established Australia as a world power in cricket was very diverse. That was its strength. The great thing about those players is that they were their own men. Players such as Border, Marsh, Boon, Waugh, Jones and Taylor all have very different personalities, but if you look at the most successful sides, you don't strike many players who are clones of each other. Contrasts make the best teams when they share a common ambition. So you had a qualified surveyor, who had travelled a lot and moved home several times, opening the batting with a farmer. And what a combination. The players had hardness, character, ambition. They did not necessarily flaunt it but the steel showed through when it mattered. They were a very focused lot, very Australian in their dislike of failure.

Boon with a bat in his hand knew no fear. Jones, for all his showmanship, could force himself through the barriers and make a life-threatening double century; Steve Waugh, tough and afraid of no-one, was a man who would eventually stare down the imposing Curtly Ambrose in Trinidad. Healy made a big difference to the side. A talker on the field like Steve Waugh, and a bloke ready to go to any lengths to play for Australia, his first tour of Pakistan became a nightmare for him, but his outstanding performances afterwards said so much about his character. The setbacks on that first tour just made him all the more determined to prove he could do the job long term.

In my opinion, the biggest mistake we made as selectors was picking Victoria's Wayne Phillips to play in the last Test of the series against India in 1991–92. Wayne had been making runs and several good judges were sure he was ready, but I did not go along with his selection because at that time it seemed like too much of a one-off. Our policy had been to give players an extended run and Phillips' selection went against that strategy. It seemed to me that Wayne was a player to watch for the future, but it was pointless — and unfair to him — to show our hand. He was on a hiding to nothing in the circumstances and the Test really didn't prove a great deal to anybody (he made 8 and 14 and never played for Australia again). The decision was made no easier by the fact that Geoff Marsh had to be dropped in order to fit Phillips in. When I went to that selection meeting, I knew Swampy probably shouldn't survive, but it was still a tough one. My hardest one of all. Geoff took it like a gentleman and, as an Australian selector himself, later faced a couple of tough decisions — not least in 1995–96 with the dropping of his best mate, David Boon.

I would never ask Geoff what his part was in that decision, but I know he will have anguished about it. If a selector hasn't got a real feeling for the players he should not be a selector. Loyalty and a belief in the players are part of the picture where selection is concerned; it does not warp your judgments, but it is not a factor you simply toss aside in order to appear strong and ruthless. The level-headed players realise it is all part of the balance of their lives and the ones who worry me are those who think they are never going to be left out. All the years I played first-class cricket I always checked to see if I was in the team. Nothing was taken for granted. Some players are not objective about their performance, they fool themselves and they are the ones who ultimately find rejection hardest to take.

Every player leaves the team eventually. This will become a much bigger issue for selectors in the future than it used to be now that the trend is for players to hang on until their 'use-by' date and beyond. It is not just the money that keeps players going today, although this is a consideration which affects families and lifestyle and is not exactly irrelevant. More significantly, cricketers are kept fitter than they were so they feel they can face one more season. Also, the tendency for players to give it away in their early to mid 30s, to develop a business career, has diminished as players now budget their career-earnings wisely. So, selectors will be faced with an increasing need to say: 'Sorry, we know you'd like to go on and you probably could, but it's time...'

This type of judgment will always be a tough one for selectors to make and there will inevitably be plenty of room for disagreement before such a decision is reached. However, the fact is somebody will have to make that judgment more and more often. In my opinion, the thing that determines the validity of omitting a still-serviceable player has to be his replacement. The selectors must get that right, yet we have all seen examples of players being grabbed in hope and lasting five minutes.

In recent seasons the Australian selectors have faced some very tough calls. I thought Allan Border went on a season too long but that David Boon was dropped at least a season too early. Dean Jones had a very good average when he was left out of the side, but his performances were not good match by match. Dean was finding new ways of getting out, which suggested his powers of concentration were deserting him. Concentration is the first thing to go, not eyesight or mobility or courage. That and the desire to be out there every day in the middle of a dogfight, to drag yourself back into the contest and play with the same single-mindedness which made you an international in the first place. It's always getting harder.

I have found that age is not the primary factor in the a cricketer's decline. Some of the oldest people I have known were 21 and I have met some young 60-year-olds. Mental attitude, form, fitness, zest for the game... these are attributes which decline without players being really aware of it. The loss of those qualities may not yet be reflected in a veteran player's average but they are the telling signs which a coach and selectors have to look for. And it comes to everybody in the end.

CHAPTER 3

It's cool!

We live in an age where it's no longer cool to appear enthusiastic. Worldly-wise is okay, blase is fine. 'Been there, done that' is the order of the day. Enthusiasm looks suspiciously like youthfulness and is shunned, particularly by young people. That is true right throughout society and is noticeable in cricket, even at a very high level. The young men who hit the first-class teams these days are as enthusiastic about the game as they ever were, but it is considered a bit ordinary to show it. Remember the ribbing Michael Slater took when he celebrated his Test century at Lord's in 1993 — punching the air and planting a big kiss on the Australian badge on his helmet. 'I did carry on a bit, didn't I?' he said apologetically afterwards. Yet the public loved it and *Wisden* even recorded: 'The exuberant display of joy enchanted a capacity crowd as much as his fleet-footed strokeplay.' Quite right, too.

One of the most overtly enthusiastic players in the Australian dressing room in recent years is Justin Langer; he loves the game and he doesn't mind letting everyone around him know the fact. The result is that he invariably cops a ribbing from the rest of the players, good-natured enough, but a sign of the times nonetheless. Justin isn't over the top as far as I am concerned, he just projects his love of the game in a very natural way and it would be a huge pity if that sort of thing was drummed out of the game.

Helping modern players be as natural as possible under a very demanding media spotlight was the thinking behind a whole new initiative aimed at preparing players for public appearances and helping them handle a high media profile. Some might scoff and dismiss the whole idea as a sort of charm school, the media were certainly sceptical when they found that Australian players were being coached in media skills and public relations. However, the demands on players these days are greater than they have ever been, the media are more intrusive and, whether they like it or not, badly-handled interviews and poor television images do a player no good at all.

If we are going to tell players that they have a responsibility to respond to public interest, the least we can do is help them respond articulately. It is not brainwashing and neither is it aimed at producing a cliched set of safe responses to media questioning.

This training program which players undertake is designed to give them greater confidence in interviews and to make their answers more interesting. It is also intended to help them avoid the curly question which can be turned, via a bit of journalistic licence, into a major controversy. Dealing with the media is just one more of a modern player's skills and I think the course has done most of them a power of good; the present generation is as good as any I have seen at handling publicity.

I remember as a young bloke I used to follow the Davis Cup tennis and was always impressed by the way the American players spoke so confidently while our lads searched for words and looked uncomfortable. Lew Hoad and Ken Rosewall, Australia's two young champions, were brilliant tennis players but they could not match the Americans for self-projection. There was, of course, something attractive in that, but they clearly felt themselves in an alien environment once the microphones were switched on. No modern sports person can afford that.

In the end it probably boils down to confidence and that means knowing yourself and knowing your subject. Surprising as it may seem, I feel a lot of today's young players lack confidence in public because they don't really have a grounding in the folklore and the history of the game. Some do, but a majority have been raised through television and the 60-second grab; they have probably never read a coaching manual much less a history of cricket. Books were knowledge before television took over and like most of my contemporaries, I received hours of pleasure out of thumbing through a battered volume on the history and techniques of the game. I used to pay two shillings for the NSW Cricket Association's yearbook and read it until the print wore off the pages — records, player profiles, the lot.

By the time I was 12, I knew all about the old players and thought I knew all about how to play the standard strokes. It didn't really make me a better cricketer but it gave me a grounding in the game which stood me in good stead. Today's youngsters home in on the television and often miss out on the wisdom and companionship of books. Their cricket education is neglected in that sense and I'm sure they would be better equipped to handle the demands that come with fame if they knew more.

One spin-off from the communication sessions is that players are looking for more information, for new ideas. It is an area they had no real reason to explore before, but they seem to take to it pretty quickly. Some quicker than others, I may say, and the coaching sessions are pretty tough. It's not easy to stand in front of a load of your mates and be told that you've made an absolute fool of yourself. A typical exercise recreates a TV studio situation, where an interviewer fires questions and a player answers them as best he can — in the knowledge that his mates will assess his performance afterwards.

The questions are not all user-friendly. 'What do you think of Bob Simpson. I believe he gives you a very bad time?' is one example. Or: 'Where do you stand on this latest demand by the players for more money. Unreasonable, isn't it?' The questions come thick and fast and the player, totally unrehearsed, has to field them as he would in a live television interview. In the real world, it's no good saying afterwards that you didn't really mean what you said.

After the interview, the sequence is replayed and the victim assesses his own performance. Then the rest of the players have their say.

Mark Taylor used to rattle away at a million miles an hour and the players soon picked up on the need for him to take it more slowly. Ian Healy was so anxious to begin his reply that he invariably cut the interviewer off in mid-question. Then he would head off at an enthusiastic tangent until nobody could remember what the original question was. This was all great fun and good team therapy, but there was a serious point at issue: if the players have to give interviews they might as well avoid the pitfalls and learn how to handle them well. And, believe me, it's not easy.

Taylor and Healy certainly come over well in interviews now; both can handle the situation confidently in their different ways. Everybody has a different interview response and there's no question of trying to make such responses dull or uniform, quite the opposite. A bloke like Glenn McGrath doesn't need a lot of on-camera tuition; he's a tall, angular man with a great 'TV face' — whatever that is. However, it can't do him any harm at all to have a better understanding of what cameras are about and how to use them, rather than let them manipulate him. It may be peripheral to his job as a fast bowler, but it is one of the extra skills which the modern professional cricketer is well advised to learn.

Previous generations got by without this sort of tuition because they had to. In any case, there wasn't the media exposure for most players that there is nowadays. Even so, I know I would have benefited enormously from some sort of media coaching when I became captain of Australia. Before the 1964 England tour, I realised I suddenly had the additional responsibility of representing the team and the country in public.

Captains nowadays get a bit of relief from speech-making because they have the back-up of tour managers, but in those days it was regarded as very much the captain's responsibility to front up at functions and it could be quite intimidating. My idea of preparing myself media-wise was to practise speeches on tape and then accept a speaking engagement a day for something like 30 days, just to gain experience. The captain was committed to some 12 speeches in 14 days when we got to England so I knew I'd have to be ready before we set off.

I'd had some experience in Australia, having taken over as captain from Richie Benaud during the series against South Africa, and I really thought I had fallen on my feet after my first speech at a Australian Cricket Board of Control dinner in Melbourne. After I sat down, a familiar voice, probably the most famous in Australia, said: 'Well done Bob. That was fine.' Quite a compliment coming from Sir Robert Menzies, but I wasn't overly happy with myself and told him how nervous I'd felt. 'You haven't done a lot of this sort of thing. If you want any help, let me know.' he replied. And when I took him at his word he sent me a whole swag of anecdotes and yarns which he had told on cricket occasions. Armed with that, how could I fail?

Trouble was, during the tour the whole lot were pinched from my bag in the dressing room at Lord's. I've no idea who did it, but one day I'll nail the bloke who's going round the speaking circuit telling Bob Menzies stories.

Official functions on tour tended to be a lot more formal in those days, of course, especially in England where there was a lot of ritual involved. We dined in extraordinary splendour, unlikely as it may sound, in the Fishmongers' Hall, having been ushered in by the Queen's Herald. Lots of 'M'Lords, ladies and gentlemen, pray silence'... That sort of thing. As I remember it, the first speech I made as captain in England was at the Sportsmen's Association at the Savoy, every bit as plush and posh and plummy as it sounds. Following speakers such as the Duke of Edinburgh or the Duke of Norfolk or the Chief Justice wasn't easy but in my case at least, it was a time-saver. The Master of Ceremonies would introduce them with all their ranks and titles and badges of office; it seemed to take half an hour. Then he'd get to me. 'And Mr R. B. Simpson ...'

Tradition insisted I had to introduce the team and I would always announce our little left-arm spinner, Johnny Martin, as the 'Mayor of Burrell Creek'. Sounded a bit impressive in the company. Johnny would stand up and give a run-down of his career, probably with reference to his civic duties. As far as I know Burrell Creek had a population of around 90 at the time and Johnny ran the local post office. The guests at the back of this enormous ballroom area couldn't actually see little Johnny so I insisted he stand on a chair; great fun and also, I think, a great vehicle for meeting people at close quarters. Some of the functions were stuffy as hell, but most were great social occasions where you developed friendships which lasted way beyond your playing days. It was learning PR skills by the seat of your pants and we all got a lot out of it.

The accent on formal dinners has weakened considerably over the years and there is nothing wrong with that, but I think some modern players miss out on an experience they would enjoy. It became fashionable to regard the formal cricket function as an imposition and a waste of time; the so-called worldly players would lounge around and make a point of looking extremely bored. Even today, players are liable to react to peer pressure and express a reluctance to get involved in the more formal occasions. I think they enjoy them when they happen but it's cool to pretend otherwise. Yet I have never known a single player who wasn't excited by the experience of meeting the Queen at Lord's. Some might pretend a certain disinterest, afraid, perhaps, of being accused of the old cultural cringe. But they put on their blazers, arrange for some privileged bystander to take a photograph for them and then badger the official photographers for a picture of the moment when they actually shake hands. Although they might appear to put on a blase front, they actually get a real kick out of the occasion. And why not?

EVERY PLAYER NEEDS TO KNOW HIS IMPORTANCE TO THE TEAM AND HIS ROLE IN IT. After all, cricket has traditionally prided itself on being the ultimate team game, the builder of character through working for others. This is partly true, partly not. However, every player has a role and in a well-structured, well-balanced team that role perfectly suits his particular abilities. There should be no need to tell a player his role in so many words; he will have been selected because he has strengths and he will be at his best — and doing his best for the team — when he plays to them.

Geoff Marsh in the one-day situation was a classic example of the player whose talents fitted perfectly into the team around him. Geoff averaged around 56 runs per 100 balls, which is not huge by limited-overs standards, but he had the ability to stay and make big scores. We knew that if he did, we had every chance of winning the match. That was his job and he did it wonderfully well in a way which suited the make-up of the side, which during his career probably played one-day cricket better than any other side has ever played the game. Individuals do not become robots just because they fit into the structure of a side but they usually do the team job better if they know just what is expected of them and are confident they can handle it.

That is one reason Australia beat the West Indies in the Caribbean in 1995 — we made the very best use of the talent we had available. The bowlers discussed their roles, their aims and their methods down to very fine detail and rarely departed from the team plan. In the end, I reckon we got 60 or 70 per cent of our wickets the way we had planned to take them and that is a hell of a return for ability and discipline. It was as fine a display of consistent, controlled bowling as I have seen. Normally you discuss, plan and devise strategies, and then they don't work precisely because bowlers deviate from the plan. However, the West Indies tour was a classic example of players knowing just where they fitted into the structure of the game and having the skill and patience to see it through.

I often make the point when I'm addressing motivational-type seminars for companies that everybody has to have a part in the plan and know what it is. The individual is important no matter how big the team. The telephonist, for instance, is the first company link with the public; the typist produces letters which will help others form an opinion of the writer. People in jobs like those sometimes tell me they are just a telephonist or just a typist, but they shouldn't be allowed to think that way. There is no such thing in a cricket team as a player who is just a bowler, just a batsman, or just a fielder. Everybody is part of the structure we call a team and they should be proud of that. There is no better motivation in life than pride in what you do and what you are.

Structure also means balance and there is a role in the game, now and in the future, for every sort of player. Cricket has to move with the times and, professionally at least, provide the public with what they want. That means closeness of matches, people being busy on the field; it means action, excitement, skill and entertainment.

Above all, it means winning. The quickest way to lose public support in Australia is to lose matches; no matter how many swashbuckling players you have, interest dies if the team is not winning. That brings us back to balance because you simply could not field a team of six Michael Slaters or six Mark Taylors, fine players that they both are in their own way.

No player won more matches off his own bat than Doug Walters; he might chip in with two or even one great innings during a Test series but it would usually win the match and that makes him an outstanding asset to any side. But there again, you could not field a side which included six Doug Walters because he would be the first to admit he needed different sorts of players around him. Solid and consistent players need to be mixed with expressive, adventurous ones. The structure is vital. History shows that you rarely find two batsmen in a partnership both scoring at a fast rate; standing instruction is that if one player is going really well, the other feeds him the strike. If it's done well, and if both players have the skill to play their roles, then the scoreboard ticks over and there is action and movement all the time.

Plenty of entertainment in that.

Let's face it, being in the public eye is not easy. A young man with a special skill for playing sport cannot become a smooth media performer overnight, even if he sometimes feels inadequate because he feels uncomfortable. Being confronted by a table-setting which involves a canteen of cutlery and half a dozen crystal glasses is definitely off-putting at first. If in doubt, work in from the outside. And keep a weather eye on the bloke next door who probably goes to six banquets a week. Blokes whose cricket small talk has been confined to grip, stance and backlift are suddenly expected to make polite conversation with total strangers as though they have done nothing else all their lives. Hard luck if they are a bit shy or tongue-tied.

It can be quite a strain and it may be even harder for the modern generation than it was for us. Have you ever tried developing the art of conversation in a disco? Nobody talks, for heavens sake.

A few years ago we banned the use of personal earphones in the Australian team, a move which was greeted with a fair bit of outrage at the time, but which has long been accepted as a move towards better communication between the players. It was that New Zealand tour in 1986, and the team was at its lowest ebb, especially since Allan Border had gone public with a threat to resign as captain unless the team pulled its socks up. The mood in the camp was pretty sombre, to say the least, and I noticed there was a distinct lack of communication among the side.

One reason, it seemed to me, was the fashion for plugging into individual Walkmans, which provided a strong insulation from the dressing-room atmosphere and the rest of the team. It was no good and I told the players so: 'Nobody says a damned word to anyone, you don't discuss the match or try to boost the confidence of those who are struggling. When you get out you pull on those damned headphones and sulk in private. A player battling the nerves of waiting to bat looks round and finds his mate has tuned into the Walkman and out of the match. It has to stop.'

The players were pretty rebellious at first, but the message got home and the atmosphere round the team certainly picked up. Nowadays, a player will probably ask if it's okay to tune into his headphones. This is not just a courtesy to the others but an important team convention as well.

Communication within the team and also outside it are very much a part of the highly-publicised modern game. The days when players were left to sink or swim has long gone; the more relaxed and comfortable a player feels with his general situation the more likely he is to perform at his best. Industry and commerce recognise this with all sorts of training courses, so there's no reason for sport to ignore the benefits. Australian cricket has made a start and I'm sure the whole field of media-PR-social counselling will become even more important in seasons to come.

Modern professionals can earn a lot of money, attractive opportunities abound and the need for sound advice in all sorts of fields has never been greater. A young bloke like Tasmania's brilliant batsman Ricky Ponting, for instance, has a wonderful career ahead of him and the chance of making a small fortune at the game.

However, his commitment to the game is such that he's never had a real job outside cricket and he knows he is not very well-equipped to handle the business side of his affairs. Suddenly he has access to a lot of money and, if he is not careful, it will run through his fingers. He, like other budding champions coming through at an early age, needs advice to avoid such pitfalls. Some will be shrewd with their money, some silly. Some will gamble it away, others will be careful to make it work for them.

The important thing is that they have access to the advice they need and are able to develop as many life-skills as possible. Being well-heeled and well-adjusted must be pretty cool.

The naturals

One of the great charms of any sport is the opportunity it gives people to succeed whether they have been blessed with huge natural talent or are just prepared to work really hard to reach the top. Not everybody is a genius, in fact most of us fall a long way below, but sport gives everybody a chance. What it encourages and rewards is individuality — and there are always a few names who spring to mind as naturals. The lucky ones, perhaps, the ones who did it their way and succeeded handsomely.

Over the years I have been asked many times whom I consider the best player I've ever seen and I confess I've always avoided a straight answer — simply because it is practically impossible to compare players of different eras. There are too many factors involved to make a simple comparison. How would Dennis Lillee have got on bowling against Bradman? How would Brian Lara have fared against Frank Tyson? How do you compute the quality of the opposition, the sort of pitches around at the time and the various changes in the laws over the years which have clearly affected the way players approach the game? It's too hard. What you can do is enjoy players in their era and take great satisfaction from the knowledge that you have seen a great player of his time.

IN the 40-odd years that I have been involved in first-class cricket I have never seen a bowler with as much natural talent as Shane Warne.

Just how a bowler like Shane came along in the modern era is something of a mystery in itself. The game worldwide had undergone a whole catalogue of changes to the laws which were not designed to encourage a leg-spinner. The accent was very much on quick cricket and fast bowlers, the environment was almost hostile to any bowler who did not set out to bowl like the wind or prevent the opposition from scoring runs. Yet, in the middle of all that emerged a thoroughly modern kid with a flair for leg-spin bowling which borders on genius. His impact has already been incalculable and it will be a pleasure to watch cricket for the next generation just to see how far he can develop. Shane can set his own limits.

Not only has he got enormous talent but he is also a modern youth in every sense of the word — earrings, dyed blond hair, the lot. His extrovert approach to the game makes a huge impact on the younger generation and fascinates older, more conservative cricket lovers with his extraordinary skills. So, in one dynamic package the Australian game and world cricket at large have discovered a player who bridges generations and culture gaps. And more than that, he is a player whose stardom is based squarely on the fact that he is an exceptional performer. Somebody up there obviously likes cricket.

Shane's ability to put fierce spin on the ball may have been matched by others over the years — perhaps by the South Australian left-arm wrist-spinner of the '60s, David Sincock, or maybe by that left-arm spinning phenomenon of the 1930s, Leslie 'Chuck' Fleetwood-Smith. However, I doubt if anybody ever spun it harder. I'm sure nobody spun the ball as much and achieved Shane's accuracy. That is one key to his unique impact on the game, the other is his ability to learn. For a bloke with so much talent, he is never deaf to a suggestion, and always willing to learn. And he absorbs lessons exceptionally quickly.

In Sri Lanka three years ago, Shane mentioned in passing that he had never bowled a top-spinner through his fingers. I showed him how to bowl it and within three weeks he was using it in a Test match — and calling it a 'zooter' if you don't mind. Some leg-spinners take seasons to perfect an unfamiliar delivery and then develop the confidence to try it in really competitive cricket; the great Richie Benaud, for example, took two or three years before he had the confidence to bowl his flipper and he was an established leggie at the time. Here, though, we had Shane unleashing his zooter after only three weeks and already practising variations!

Shane had the flipper in his armoury by the time he was 18 or so; he has a magic box of deliveries and variations — the one which spins just a little, one that's a bit slower, one that hurries on. Now you see it, now you don't. It really is an amazing store of knowledge, but there is just a danger that Shane may overbowl his derivations and variations rather than concentrating on basics with surprises thrown in. He has enough sense to avoid that, but only time will tell.

Shane has exceptionally strong hands and fingers. Standing where the bowler's umpire stands, it really is amazing: you can hear the ball fizzing out of his hands and displacing the air as it spins down the pitch. I have worked with a few spinners in my time and I recall bowlers like Johnny Martin who really put a lot on the ball, but I've never heard the ball hum out of the hand as it does when Shane gets it right. It is intimidating from the bowler's end; goodness only knows what the batsmen think.

Spinning the ball so hard means that Shane gets exceptional zip and bounce off the pitch and also has the ability to make the ball dip sharply in flight. He often bowls round the wicket these days, a particularly useful addition to the armoury which he developed after long discussions in Perth some years ago. I tried to convince him that bowling round the wicket could be a very valuable asset, but he wasn't impressed. So, every night after a Test match in New Zealand, we'd go into the nets, Shane as the batsman and me bowling modest leg-spin. He was hopeless, he couldn't handle it at all — and the role reversal convinced him that going round the wicket was worth learning. Once he had accepted it he worked typically hard at getting it right and on the 1993 Ashes tour used it brilliantly as both an attacking and a defensive ploy. Shane has only been in the game for five minutes and I bet he has already dismissed more batsmen from round the wicket than any other bowler in a career. He's a quick learner.

Possessing so much natural ability is all the more amazing in Shane's case because there is nothing natural about mastering leg-spin bowling. It's a pain. The physical demands are high, technique has to be well-nigh perfect or the body will rebel. It looks pretty easy — Shane walking a few paces back and a few paces in, a brief flurry of activity — but physically it is a real ordeal. The strains on the back, shoulders, wrist and fingers — all subjected to an unnatural twisting action — are extreme. Until 1996 Shane hasn't had too much trouble with his fingers and that is a rarity in itself; most spinners develop splits, calluses and general wear areas. Benaud and Jim Higgs did, Tim May among modern spinners is a classic example of the calloused nature of the trade. Shane, however, has little trouble and for a bloke who spins the ball so hard, that is amazing. Most of the non-calloused spinners are the ones who didn't spin the ball enough to matter.

Shane will have to work hard on his fitness. He is no greyhound and if he lets his fitness level drop his energy level will follow. Without explosive energy, he will lose the ability to spin the ball prodigiously and accurately at the same time. But he is aware of the dangers, the pitfalls and the rewards.

As a bloke, he's a gem to have around. Sure, he likes a drink and a night out, he's a bit of a punter and a real ocker in many ways, but with more sophistication than most. It can be argued that no cricketer in this country has had more media attention focused on him — bearing in mind the absence of television and intrusive media fashions when many greats made their name — but he takes the pressures in his stride. He lost it in South Africa in 1994 and was quite rightly fined heavily, but he usually handles the stardom thing very well. He is very polite and considerate, and particularly good with kids. Shane is also quite an accomplished magician — card tricks, coins, peas in the ear — which owes a lot to manual dexterity and therefore should be no surprise. And, above all, he is intelligent. Some people insist you have to be an idiot to want to be a leg-spinner and there are easier ways of earning a living, for sure. But it is a thinking man's game, so Shane has a head start.

The only problem I see with Shane Warne at the moment is boredom. He does get bored sometimes and you can see his enthusiasm and energy levels drop; it's the only time I've sensed a danger for him. However, he has too much pride to allow that to get to a stage where it becomes cricket-life-threatening. We are always debating the future of the game, the quality and class of players needed to carry it through, and Warne fits the bill well into the next century. Why wouldn't he? He is all class.

LOOK at English cricket in recent years and you have to think of somebody like David Gower, a man with extraordinary natural ability in just about every area of the game, but a cricketer who, although he would deny it until he was blue in the face, never really thought a lot about the game. David hates the idea that he went through his career being laid-back, a little offhand. However, having watched him at close quarters, particularly when he was an adversary playing for England, I can promise you that David's reputation was well deserved. It is not necessarily a criticism, but it is a fact.

It showed especially in his approach to captaincy. He had a pretty quirky way of going about the job for England and he considered there was only one way of captaincy and that was his way. I have known a lot more successful captains who were far more open to suggestion than David, but as far as he was concerned, the Gower way was gospel. It was a weakness, no doubt about it, and it forms part of David's record.

But the big picture was that he was so attractive to watch as a player and so talented — very close to genius class — that nobody seriously doubts his contribution to the game. When you unearth a diamond, you sometimes have to overlook the flaws.

As a batsman, there was nothing David could not do. He was a freak. He had a wonderful ability to time the ball and pick gaps in the field, there was a gracefulness about him that was almost feminine yet he had great strength and power. It must have been an illusion, but David actually seemed to move more slowly than other batsmen — he called one of his early books *With Time to Spare* and that always summed him up. His positioning was usually perfect which means he was picking up the ball very early, much quicker than any other batsman around at the time.

And look at him in the field. He probably does not appreciate to this day just how brilliant a fieldsman he was, but those of us who watch and analyse could only marvel at him. I have seen many outstanding fieldsmen in my time and David was unquestionably one of the best.

The greatest cover and midwicket fielders share an uncanny and uncoachable ability to pick the shortest distance to the ball. The mental computer works out speed, angle and distance in a flash, the co-ordination between eyes and brain and legs is perfect, the fielder moves intuitively to where the ball is going to be. There must be some sort of radar involved and woe betide the batsman who underestimates it; world-class fielders save dozens of runs simply because batsmen are too cautious to take them on. The ball is fizzing away, the angle is impossible and then you see a Gower moving in from the corner of your eye. He should miss it, but you never know… you just never know.

David had a distinctive fielding style in that he was one of the very few fieldsmen I have seen who approached the batsman at an odd angle. Most cover fielders, even the very good ones, walk towards the batsman in a straight line, which seems logical enough, but means they tend to arrive at fielding positions square of the ball, with their shoulders pointing through the line of the stroke. However fast they get there, they are not in the best position to change direction with the ball in their hands.

I don't know if he was aware of it, but David always walked in on a line that would have taken him a yard in front of the batsman at the crease. He could spring left or right easily, and cover more distance without breaking stride. So many cover fieldsmen begin their approach with the bowler and stop, just momentarily, as the batsman plays his stroke. David never actually stopped; he reacted, adjusted his stride and, because he was an absolute genius at picking the angle, he seemed to cover twice as much territory. His movements were unbroken, as graceful in their way as his batting style. Graceful Gower… the unmistakable image.

He should have been more stimulated by day-to-day cricket, but, like many naturals, he seemed to find it a bit irksome. What came easily to him, he expected to come easily to others, and he certainly gave no sort of a lead as far as organising nets or practice was concerned. It is revealing that he averaged 38 for Leicestershire in the English county championship and 44 internationally for England — the clear fingerprint of a man stimulated by the big time and, like so many naturals, dogged by a low threshold of boredom.

SPEAKING of which, there is Ian Botham. Talk of flair, individuality, a flash of genius here and there, and you cannot escape him; Australia certainly couldn't in 1981. Not many series have been dominated by an individual in the way that Botham won England the Ashes that year. It was more than a little ironic, when you consider that Botham is probably as un-English a player as you'd ever see. In terms of attitude and approach to the game, Botham was an old-fashioned Australian all-rounder.

England has not produced many like him, but the mould is much more familiar in Australia — Keith Miller, Alan Davidson, Richie Benaud, Ronnie Archer and the rest. Robust, aggressive, super-confident players who went after everything and never knew when they were beaten. Botham was often dismissed as a braggart or a disruptive influence in England, even when he was winning Test matches virtually on his own. Sure, he went over the top; he lived on the edge as far as the Establishment was concerned and there's no doubt he brought a good deal of pain on himself. But he was a hell of a player.

Ian had a lot to say for himself and frequently about himself, but I don't think he was fully aware of his huge ability, in the technical sense, as a batsman. I was astounded that when he found he could no longer make the grade as a Test bowler he did not hold down a place in the England side as a batsman; it certainly was not for want of talent. The myth grew that Botham was a big muscular bloke with a good eye and a railway sleeper for a bat who simply blasted his way out of trouble whatever the circumstances — a sophisticated slogger if you like. However, there was a very polished technician behind the smokescreen.

Given his temperament, Ian would probably scoff at that idea. He liked to portray the image of pure, uncluttered genius at work, a natural untainted by the coaching manual. A free spirit. Some of it, of course, was perfectly true, and it is probably just as well that he never learned discretion, otherwise he would have rewritten the records faster than they could be printed. He was a man driven by his temperament; it sometimes let him down but that's the price naturals have to pay.

Early in his international career, at least, Botham's bowling was smooth and rhythmic. It was said throughout his career that he probably took more wickets with bad balls than anybody else in the game, but that was just a reflection of his aggressive approach and a useful tool in promoting his image. Botham's bowling came naturally and easily, but it was much closer to technical excellence than a lot of people appreciate. He had genuine pace and bounce, and was a rarity in his era in that he swung the ball both ways; until he put on weight he had everything the Test bowler needs. In the field he was a big man, but remarkably agile and with highly-tuned reflexes. He drove some of the critics to distraction with his habit of waiting in the slips with his hands plonked on his thighs but he didn't drop many and some of his better catches were out of this world.

Above all, Botham was one of those characters who takes the game by the short and curlies, and makes it go his way. I'd put him in the Doug Walters class of player; someone who actually wins matches and there is no higher praise than that. Botham was frightened of nobody and nothing was beyond him. At least, nothing he was prepared to admit.

Significantly, Botham averaged a modest 21 against the West Indies and I suspect that, for once, his macho image worked against him. Confronted by the best side in the world at the time, he felt he had to personally take up the challenge. Here was a statement about his own status in world cricket. He wanted to hook to show that he was superior and unafraid, he wanted to attack to show that he could not be intimidated. The West Indies bowling attack, however, was a bit too good for him to approach matches in this way; he would never admit that, but the figures do not lie. The qualities which made him such a dynamic performer would not allow him to threaten his image by changing his approach.

A lot of natural players face that problem. They develop a huge image for confidence and self-determination which they have to live up to. And that's doubly difficult when the opposition's reputation and ego are as big as your own. I suspect that against the West Indies, Ian knew deep down he had met his match. A lot of his bluster and bravado was aimed at building his confidence and he sounded far more assured than he felt. He always struck me as being forced to live up to an image which became larger than life.

In the end, he became a bit larger than he could handle. As a natural performer Botham tended to underestimate the need for fitness; he was strong and technically sound, and that kept him going for a long time at the top. However, his lack of condition crept up on him, his waistline expanded and as he got older, his body became less forgiving. The strain on his back became obvious; he could not hold the firm bowling positions which help to prevent injury and he finally had to submit to back surgery. However willing, he was never the same player again. Perhaps it could have been prevented with a different lifestyle and workstyle but then world cricket might have missed something special. With naturals, you never know.

ONE of the great delights of my career was to watch Dougie Walters, whether he was batting, bowling or fielding. Walters was the epitome of the great unorthodox player, and he was an engaging character who developed a wonderful relationship with cricket followers despite never playing to the crowd. On and off the field, Dougie was a natural.

It is hard to know where to start with Dougie. A century between lunch and tea against West Indies, perhaps? Or between tea and stumps against England? An inspired piece of fielding, a change bowler who broke the unbreakable stand? Dougie did it all in a long career and left the game as he started it — unassuming, undemonstrative, as happy with a beer and a cigarette as he was with a Test century and a match-winning performance. There have been precious few like him.

It amazes me that Dougie did not perform well in England because, frankly, batting on good English pitches is the easiest batting in the world. He made four tours to England and never scored a Test century, a career statistic which will always rankle with those who appreciate just how magnificent a player he was. It has been suggested that his record in England highlights some basic flaw in Dougie's technique. That is pure rubbish; he had everything a batsman needs to succeed, in England or anywhere else. Perhaps the English bowlers simply bowled better to Doug in England than they did in Australia. In England, they bowled intelligently round about off stump, where every batsman is at his most vulnerable. When they came to Australia, they tended to get carried away by the extra pace and bounce of the pitches and seemed to imagine they could explore some weakness against the shorter ball. Doug hooked and cut them brilliantly.

The notion that Doug could have problems with the rising ball on or outside the off stump was not entirely fanciful. He had a slightly unorthodox grip which made it difficult for him to get his hands high enough to deal with the shorter stuff, but it was never enough of a problem to represent a major weakness. In any case, this would not apply to any great extent in England so it doesn't explain his lack of success there. Nor does the idea that he was vulnerable to the ball swinging or moving off the seam, a favourite theory of English experts when they want to see shortcomings in any visiting batsman, hold up.

One of the biggest myths about cricket in England is the amount of movement off the seam which bowlers are supposed to create there. You might get that on a badly-prepared county pitch and you could probably cook up something similar anywhere in the world if you tried hard enough. However, I rarely encountered an out-and-out seamer in Test matches; the English groundsmen were proud of their craft and prepared the best possible pitch for a five-day match. Mind you, they are under more pressure these days.

Dougie's greatest strength was his ability to hit identical deliveries past point or past square leg! He didn't worry too much about technical conventions or whether a shot might seem inappropriate in the circumstances, he just went about the business of batting with an unerring eye and footwork which was simply unique. He picked up the line and length of the ball extraordinarily quickly and was never caught in 'no-man's land'. Dougie would play a long way forward or a long way back — the hallmark of a batsman who picks up the ball early — and his judgment was hard to fault. His footwork was so sure and quick that he was able to attempt strokes other batsmen would still have been thinking about. It was probably significant that in his early days he used a bat weighing around 2lb 2oz, a far cry from the fashion which developed for bats that feel like trees with the branches lopped off. Bradman and Hutton, among many great players, had a preference for light bats; these days they range up to 3lbs!

One of Walters' trademark shots was the drive through midwicket, which he played like a guardsman snapping to attention. You could hear the click of his heels coming together as he clipped the ball away. I've never seen or heard anything quite like it. And he was a brilliant batsman against the spinners, largely because he had wonderfully soft hands which enabled him to control and feel the bat without squeezing the life out of it. The bat-pad method of playing spin was in fashion but Dougie never bothered with it; there was nothing in his manual that said you had to strap bat and pad together against anyone.

When Australia went to the West Indies in 1973, they cooked a couple of pitches and reckoned that the great off-spinner, Lance Gibbs, would run through us. Australians did not have a particularly high reputation against spinners at the time and it was a real possibility. Gibbs must have fancied himself in Trinidad but Dougie was superb. He improvised, back cut, went down the pitch, made Gibbs look ordinary, scored 100 out of 130 between lunch and tea on the first day and batted with total assurance and without once relying on the bat-pad mentality. Dougie just did it his way — and Australia went on to win a famous Test match by 44 runs.

One of the great innings was played by Dougie against England in Perth in 1974–75. The pitch was quick and bouncy — Lillee and Thommo took 11 wickets between them in the match — and England's Bob Willis was in full cry at a time in his career when he was distinctly quick. Dougie was on 97 when the last ball of the second day was dug in short by Willis. That would have been enough for most batsmen… sway out of the way, wait until tomorrow. Dougie, however, stepped inside it and hooked it for six, as cool as you please. This must be one of the most remarkable strokes in Test cricket history and said a lot about the man who played it. For the record, Australia won that Test by nine wickets, with over a day to spare.

Dougie's bowling became something of a legend. He developed a reputation as a breaker of partnerships and it became a self-fulfilling prophecy; batsmen who had been going along steadily against frontline stuff took fright when Dougie came on and, sure enough, a wicket would fall. Dougie never rated his own bowling highly, but his success was no fluke. He could swing the ball dangerously in an era when there were few swing bowlers around and that's what accounted for most of his victims.

He was unquestionably the most underrated fielder of his time. In an era of many superb fieldsmen, Dougie was unobtrusive, unruffled and very, very efficient. While others were talked about a great deal, Dougie did the business. Like Gower, he had the ability to attack the ball by the shortest possible route and, more often than Gower, he hit the stumps. This is a fingertip sort of skill, a knack which some fieldsmen have and which turns an unlikely stop into a wicket-taking ability. Allan Border had it, Dougie had it — and Dougie being Dougie, of course, he made it look so damned easy.

The stories about Dougie's laid-back approach are legendary and mostly true. Burning the candle at both ends and in the middle is not a lifestyle I'd

Something you rarely see in the '90s — a sweep shot in the West Indies. This one came in early 1978, during my final tour as Australia's captain.

If I needed a wicket from one ball, and could ask any bowler I'd ever seen to bowl it for me, I would nominate Alan Davidson (top). The batsman out below is the West Indies' Lance Gibbs, caught by Wally Grout off Davo during the famous 1960–61 series. The thing that struck me about this photo was the distance between Wally and myself. We always gave each other plenty of room.

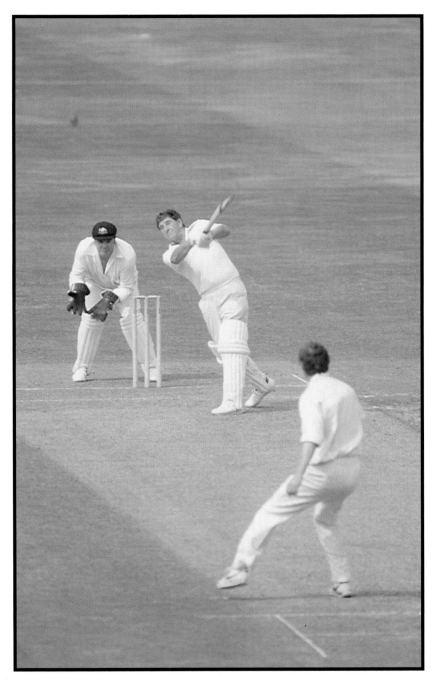

Ken Barrington goes over the top in an Old England v Old Australia game at The Oval in 1980. One of Ken's favourite tricks was to bring up his century with a six. I don't think any other Test batsman did it as often as he did.

LEFT: **Norm O'Neill's good looks and daring batting would have made him a fortune if he'd been scoring hundreds today.** RIGHT: **Bill Lawry was such a good player. I love the classic stance here, standing tall but with the knees slightly bent, head right over the line over middle stump. From this stance, he could move his body into position to play any shot, with time to spare.**

TOP LEFT: **Neil Harvey, the best all-round fieldsman I ever saw.** TOP RIGHT: **Doug Walters in the mid '60s, not long after he came into the Australian team.** ABOVE: **Dougie on a turner in Trinidad, third Test, 1973, when he improvised so magnificently that he scored a century between lunch and tea. No Australian batsman since World War II won more Tests off his own bat than Doug Walters.**

TOP LEFT: **Ian Chappell goes back and across to drive through mid on. This was certainly Ian's own style, and it worked for him, but others who tried to mimic him were much less successful.**
TOP RIGHT: **Geoff Boycott, wonderfully balanced . . . in total control.** ABOVE: **The one and only Max Walker. No other man could have bowled in this way, but Maxie took 138 Test wickets!**

Greg Chappell . . . all elegance.

Ian Botham, beating Australia with bat and ball in 1981. In both photographs, his technique is perfect. And the results that amazing summer showed just how effective he could be.

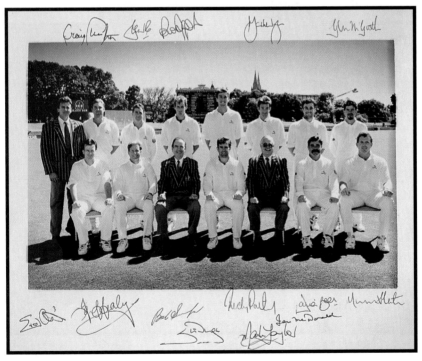

Two teams, 10 years apart. TOP: **The Australians in New Zealand in 1986.** BOTTOM: **The Australian team that beat Sri Lanka in the third Test in Adelaide in 1996, David Boon's last Test as a player . . . and mine as coach. Only three other men made both team photos.**

THIS PAGE AND NEXT: **The great Allan Border — let no-one underestimate his influence on Australian cricket.** TOP: **With the World Cup, 1987.** ABOVE: **Holding the Ashes in 1993.**

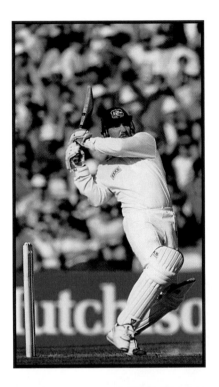

TOP LEFT: **The ultimate professional.** TOP RIGHT: **After breaking Sunil Gavaskar's Test run-scoring record in Christchurch in 1993.** ABOVE: **The fastest and deadliest throwing arm in one-day cricket history.**

TOP: **AB and I in 1986–87, our first full season together in charge of the Australian team.** ABOVE: **David Boon in Adelaide that same season, after scoring a century. Despite this effort, Boonie was struggling, and before the series was over he was out of the side . . .**

ABOVE: **But, of course, David came back to be a champion. Here he is at Lord's in 1989, where he scored 94 in the second Test.** BELOW: **Geoff Marsh, Boon's great mate and opening partner, but in many ways a very different sort of bloke. They were an odd couple, but both were so important to the Australia team.**

Steve Waugh lets himself go, full blast, in the opening game of the 1995 West Indies tour. But, nowadays, he wouldn't play this sort of shot in a Test, such is his self-control.

TOP LEFT AND RIGHT: **Two shots of Mark Waugh — one from the text-book, the other, complete improvisation. But both equally effective.** ABOVE: **Stephen (left) and Mark after our series win in the Caribbean. Off the field, despite the fact they have nothing against each other, they're rarely seen this close together.**

An Ian Healy back cut . . . must have been the first ball of his innings!

recommend, but it certainly worked for him. Even when he was just a kid, fresh onto the international scene with scores of 155 and 115 in his first two Tests (against England in 1965–66), Dougie had a reputation for liking life. Brian Booth, my vice-captain at the time, and I decided we should have a man-to-man talk with him. The wisdom of experience and all that. I can't remember if Dougie was smoking a cigarette when we sat him down but the chances are he was. 'Dougie,' we advised, 'if you're going to make it at Test level you have to look after yourself. You can't smoke as much as you do. You can't stay out most of the night . . .' He listened intently, even nodded a few times as I recall. And then went out and did his own thing. That's Dougie.

However, he was never a discipline problem. He did his own thing and nobody in the team was crazy enough to try and copy him, although a few outsiders tried to stay the pace and usually ended up broken men. There are horses that envy Doug Walters' constitution. He never said much, but he was great at the one-liners, as he still is on the speaking circuit. The bottom line was that Dougie just didn't like going to bed; if there was a companion about, Dougie would keep him company for the quiet hell of it. Beneath it all, he was shrewd and focused. He loved making runs and he loved to win. He let his performances speak for him and earned as much respect and affection as any player I have known. That, in an age before pure showmanship via television screens became more evident, was the measure of an outstanding personality. Those who met Dougie, even though it might only have been through the radio or newspaper reports, felt they knew him. And they probably did.

MODERN PLAYERS ARE FITTER THAN EVER. In fact, it has been suggested they do more physical jerks in a warm-up on the morning of a match than previous generations did all season! That would certainly be true of some old-timers — mainly batsmen — whose preparation for the season consisted of hours in the nets and a bit of running to loosen the muscles and develop a bit of stamina. They were not unfit, but the idea that they had to be super-fit never arose. It is still common to hear old-timers wonder aloud whether all the physical work makes modern cricketers better players... I don't think it makes them worse. What intrigues me is the number of injuries suffered by players acknowledged as being very fit. I wonder if it goes back to a lifestyle which once developed natural fitness and which is no longer relevant to the cricketers of today. It's a theory which gets an airing whenever I talk about fitness coaching but it strikes me as having very important implications for the future. Are the injuries professional cricketers suffer the result of too much cricket or too little training? How much training can a player take before it become counter-productive? I don't know the answer, but my gut feeling is that kids have to be reintroduced to physical training programs in primary schools because their lifestyle will not develop the sort of fitness sport requires.

I came from Marrickville, a working-class suburb in Sydney's inner west, where the lifestyle was basic and the usual form of transport was shanks' pony. My dad never had a car so there was no chance of little Simpson being dropped off at his weekend sporting event and picked up later, much less being ferried down to school or the shops. If you wanted to get somewhere, you took the train; more often, money being tight, you walked. A youngster's lifestyle was wrapped around running, jumping, climbing trees, throwing stones. There weren't so many cars around in those days so throwing stones was probably not as antisocial as it is now and there is still a pole in Illawarra Road, Marrickville, which bears the scars of the Simpson boys' throwing skills. Illawarra Road was a main thoroughfare then and it wasn't even kerbed and guttered. The lifestyle made you naturally tougher. I can't say it made you athletic but it did develop a level of robustness which a lot of kids today don't have.

Whether they can recapture this robustness in their teens, when kids with talent start thinking about sport as a career, is a debatable point. Take the gymnasts of today, who are more flexible and supple than ever before. They begin their training practically in infancy! If kids miss out on achieving a reasonable level of fitness before their teenage years, I doubt they will be able to catch up. Their body size and shape will have developed by then and so will their sense of balance, or lack of it. Balance is absolutely vital to anybody who has ambitions to do well in sport. Balance is fundamental to cricket; some players certainly look more adroit and athletic than others, but nobody without balance makes it at the highest levels.

Certainly, there's no excuse for unfit kids as far as Australia's climate and environment goes. I remember going over to England for an Ashes series and watching a group of children trying to practise before the start of the season. It was April and they were just out of a long northern winter — they looked like little old men, all white and wizened. Our kids really are lucky.

The West Indies enjoy a year-round warm climate and their cricketers always seem to be loose-limbed and flexible so I feel that climate and conditioning are not entirely unrelated. Mind you, the old work ethic counts for a lot, too. Alec Bedser bowled 15,918 deliveries for England in 51 Tests and took 236 wickets — on top of a heavy workload for his county club Surrey. Alec was always very proud of his durability as a bowler and could not understand why modern bowlers, supposedly fitter than he was, could suffer so many work-related injuries. When he went to Surrey as a rawboned young man, they got him fit for bowling — by bowling. He was told to bowl for six hours a day, not at full pace of course but at a respectable lick, and he developed a body strength which became legendary. Were Bedser and the men of his generation fitter than the international players of today? In broad terms, probably not, but Alec Bedser was tougher and more resilient. It will be very interesting to see the way sports fitness develops as the benefits of modern living make life 'easier'. 〉

SOMEBODY once described Michael Holding as the 'Rolls-Royce' of fast bowling and I can't disagree with that description. Discuss the relative pace of bowlers over the years — their effectiveness, their strike rate, whatever else is supposed to make them great players — and Michael qualifies on every count. On top of this, nobody made it look as easy as he did. Ray Lindwall was close, but, in terms of sheer style and smoothness, Michael Holding stands alone. He made fast bowling graceful and not many can lay claim to that.

I faced him once, when I was 59 (years not runs) and he still had that amazing rhythmic run, that apparently effortless approach to the crease which earned him international recognition as 'Whispering Death'. I'm glad to say it was in a charity match and Michael was under strict instructions from my wife not to bowl bouncers; we were both wired for sound in any case and I could hear him announcing his intentions to the commentators. 'I think I'll let him have this one between the eyes,' said Holding. 'I think I'll let the next batsman have a turn,' said Simpson. Fortunately, the threat was never followed through.

Michael Holding was theatre. Watching him from the stand was exciting, enough to make you a little breathless. Something was always going to happen and usually did. Batsmen who faced him needed real guts and spectators marvelled at the controlled menace of every delivery. The legend grew that he had been a top athlete in his youth and could have represented his native Jamaica in the Olympics, but Michael himself dismissed it. 'My partner in junior cricket was a fella called Seymour Newman, who ran in the 800 metres in the Olympics,' he once explained 'but there was never any chance of me doing that. I wasn't very good — as an athlete I was just mediocre.'

Holding never looked stretched, always gave the impression he had another metre up his sleeve and used an exceptionally long run. He was 190cm tall and wiry rather than robust, and, given his build, he did remarkably well to go through his career practically injury-free. If there was single secret to his exceptional pace it was timing — the ability to reach the crease just when his momentum was at its greatest. All the smoothness, rhythm and effectiveness of his bowling action derived from that; it was as close to perfection as you will ever see.

Another reason why Michael was such a great fast bowler was that he was so relaxed. He is an easy-going person which probably helps; I don't remember him being over-demonstrative on the field and there was certainly none of the 'playing to the gallery' which some fast bowlers have developed into a fine art. As a young Test bowler in his first Test series, in 1975–76, he spat the dummy in Sydney after an unsuccessful caught behind appeal against Ian Chappell, but there were very few moments like that in a long and demanding career. He disciplined himself and rarely allowed anything to divert him from his job.

Stress tightens muscles, we have all experienced that. Michael, however, kept himself loose and that made him flexible. He could extend himself or hold a delivery back without any apparent change in approach or delivery. He could make very subtle changes without communicating his intention to the batsman. The quicker or slower ball were both delivered without effort and he could vary his angle of delivery practically unnoticed by the batsman because there was no obvious physical strain involved. All that made him a particularly nasty proposition when the resulting delivery came out at 145kph!

Golfers know the importance of being relaxed, the apparently-contradictory relationship between physical effort and results. Lee Trevino urges us to swing 'loose as a goose' and Jack Nicklaus once remarked: 'If I want to hit the ball straight, I firm up. If I really want to hit it a long way, I loosen up completely.' Michael's fast bowling style employed the same philosophy. Timing was everything.

Given the potentially lethal power at his fingertips, it is worth noting that Michael Holding was also a genuine sportsman. I do not believe he ever bowled with the intention of injuring a batsman and he certainly never made mileage, as some have, out of his potential to spill blood. When he played for Derbyshire in England, and for Tasmania, Michael refused to bowl on dodgy pitches because he feared somebody would be seriously hurt. Not many fast bowlers have done that and it is to his enormous credit that, in circumstances some fast bowlers would have exploited ruthlessly, he refused to proceed.

WE often talk about talent, but rarely define it. By its very nature, I suppose, it is a little intangible. However, if talent means exceptional natural skills plus the ability to put them to use, then nobody exemplified the natural better than Alan Davidson. If my life depended on one delivery I'd ask 'Davo' to bowl it.

More than any bowler I have seen, speed or spin, Davo had the ability to get batsmen out. Look at his bowling record — 672 first-class wickets at 20.90 and 186 Test wickets at 20.53 in a first-class career that ran from 1949 to 1963 — and his strike record is exceptional. Records don't always tell the whole story, but in Davo's case they don't flatter his ability. Quite the opposite if anything. He spent a lot of his career in the shadow of some very fine bowlers — Keith Miller and Ray Lindwall were a bit hard to displace with the new ball! — and he tended to be a bit underrated in pedigree company. But Alan Davidson carried Australia's bowling in the second half of his career and there's no doubt that for some time he was the best new-ball bowler in the world.

Davo had everything. A big man with strong, broad shoulders, he was nevertheless amazingly quick and flexible — as good a fieldsman in his early days as you will ever see. Reflex catches at short leg and in the slips, great speed over the ground, a bullet arm. Later in his career, Alan developed a shoulder complaint which restricted his throwing ability without affecting his bowling, but until then I rated him as a fieldsman alongside Neil Harvey. And 'Harv' was the best all-round fieldsman I ever saw.

Davidson was unquestionably one of the greatest strike bowlers in the game, a prodigious swinger of the ball whose natural line and movement probably deceived more top-class batsman than any other bowler in memory. Englishman Tommy Graveney shouldering arms in Melbourne and lbw for a duck, Roy McLean of South Africa shouldering arms twice — bowled off stump first time and leg stump the second! Those images linger because they were wonderful triumphs of a bowler's technique over a proven batsman's ability.

The interesting thing about Davo's bowling was that he never tried to swing the ball away. The inswinger was his natural delivery and when the ball left the bat it was because of the angle of the delivery, not because of outswing. That gave Davo a huge advantage because it meant he could bowl the same line for his inswinger and the one which went on with the arm. There was nothing in his action to suggest which delivery would swing and which one wouldn't; he simply held the ball slightly differently.

Most right-handed bowlers fall away a little bit when they try to bowl the inswinger. You see them do it and know what's coming. Most left-handers fall away a little trying to bowl the outswinger and you pick it. However, Davo didn't alter his line or action. Very awkward… just ask Graveney or McLean or a whole lot of other Test-class batsmen. Davo's always pitched the ball up to allow it to swing. The skill and geometry of his bowling were fascinating, easily the best bowling of its type I've ever seen. It was pure deception at a very respectable pace. It is always said that left-armers are not as quick as right-arm bowlers and there may be statistics to prove that, but Davo bowled a bouncer sharply enough to make the batsman wish he hadn't. In his early days he was pretty challenging — not in the Lillee, Thomson or Lindwall mould, but getting on that way — and later in his career he was fast rather than express. Quick enough to be awkward and cunning enough to deceive the best batsmen around.

It was an education just to watch experienced batsmen embarrassed by the delivery which went away. Sensational, as long as you weren't at the receiving end. Batsmen who should have known better ended up playing at balls a foot outside the off stump, knowing that they simply could not work him out. They'd frown, shake their heads and offer a look that said: 'What the hell am I doing out here?' As wicketkeeper and first slip, Wally Grout and I had a birds' eye view of Davo at work and probably took one-third of the total catches that came from his bowling.

Davo still has a great passion for the game and has given enormous service to NSW and Australian cricket. He will demonstrate his grip and style at the drop of a bread roll and is always ready with advice for any bowler wise enough to ask. A few years ago, an up-and-coming left-arm quick named Mike Whitney was bowling at a single stump before a match at Newcastle, pounding them down without much success, when Davo came along and offered his advice. 'Better still, why don't you show me?' said Whitney. So, 20 years after his retirement, Davo took off his jacket, swung a delivery nine inches and knocked the stump out of the ground. You never lose it.

Davo spent more time on the massage table than most — given his workload why wouldn't he — and it became a friendly joke among the boys.

In Cape Town, at the end of the 1957–58 Australian tour of South Africa (my first overseas tour with the Australian team), we had a whip round and with the proceeds bought a metal plaque. Onto that plaque went the inscription, 'The A.K. Davidson Special Massage Table', and then we nailed it to the table. At the same time, somebody had a letterhead printed which read: 'Messrs Muscle, Muscle and Muscle, You Know Street, Gosford' ('You know' was a favourite Davo expression, Gosford his home town in NSW), and underneath was a letter which remarked: 'Dear Mr Davidson, we have great pleasure in enclosing our cheque for one rand as your first royalty on the A.K.D. Massage Table.'

We stood back grinning, not really knowing what Davo's reaction would be. He was so touched by our thoughtfulness that he began to cry! I imagine he still has the letter. Probably the plaque as well.

I have read the theories about why cricket balls swing and I confess I still don't really understand the physics involved. However, I know they do and I know Alan Davidson was a supreme exponent of the art. He had it all, flowing from an action which was the coaching classic, perfect for swing bowling. I reckon his action should have been captured in bronze and preserved for every new cricket generation. In that way, when anyone asked how to be a real swing bowler, the statue would have provided the model. The answer would simply be: 'Do it like Davo.'

NEIL HARVEY WAS SO ACCOMPLISHED AND VERSATILE THAT YOU COULD PUT HIM IN ANY POSITION ON THE FIELD AND HE WOULD MAKE AN ART FORM OUT OF IT. A magnificent slips fieldsman, short leg, leg slip, outfielder and of course, regarded by many as the finest cover fieldsman of all time! I have never seen anyone better at judging the angles and getting to the ball by the shortest possible route.

Many years ago I was 12th man in a Test against England in Brisbane and found myself fielding in the cover point region next door to Neil. I was a bit nippy in those days, fancied myself a bit, and I reckoned I would intercept everything in the area before Harvey had a chance to pounce. I concentrated like hell and charged in ready to spring in any direction. Neil invariably trotted in front of me, picked up the ball and flicked it to the wicketkeeper in one movement. And then gave me a very knowing look.

It took me years to work out why he was so outstanding and the answer was angles. Neil could have taught Pythagoras a thing or two; he had an extraordinary ability to compute everything in a flash and pick the quickest line to the ball. How many batsmen headed off for a reasonable-looking single and were run out by Neil moving in with a casual sort of suddenness? His speed over the ground was a factor, of course, but his secret was that ability to plot the straight line. His example helped me enormously as a coach, not least when one-day cricket became popular and it was so important to get the best out of every fieldsman on the ground. The shortest distance between two points really is a straight line; Neil Harvey proved it every time he played and I never let another generation of cricketers forget it.

〉

THERE are all kinds of naturals, just as there are all kinds of styles and temperaments. So the leap from Alan Davidson to a strikingly individualistic bowler like Jeff Thomson is not as far-fetched as it may seem. Thommo was a natural and, although a lot of play was made of a so-called one-off windmill action, the fact is that his methods were technically excellent. At the point of delivery — and this has been captured precisely in many photographs — his bowling action was perfect. The feet square to the crease, shoulders right round and a full, flowing arc… it was as good a bowling action as any professional would wish to achieve. There has been a tendency to concentrate on the distinctive nature of Thommo's style and let's face it, there have been prettier bowling actions. However, in terms of getting everything right I don't think there's been a better action in the game. The fact that Thommo bowled so effectively without ever suffering back problems says a great deal for the smoothness and efficiency of what looked like an exceptionally demanding style.

And he was fast. The fastest bowler I have ever seen and I include all the West Indians in that. Charlie Griffith ran him close for pure pace but Charlie had an interesting action, as they say. Thommo was an explosion of speed and, despite occasional gruesome evidence to the contrary, remarkably accurate. I know of no-one who could bowl as fast as he did and still achieve accuracy — especially as he was sometimes looking at point when he let the ball go! He had everything and, significantly, he did his own thing naturally. Nobody would have coached a style like that.

Thomson was a natural athlete who played high-class soccer, ran easily, took easily to golf, and was a fine fielder and thrower until he damaged his shoulder in that awful collision with opening batsman Alan Turner when they both went for a catch in the first Test of the 1976–77 home series against Pakistan. Thommo wrecked his right shoulder in that incident and missed the rest of that series, a tour to New Zealand, and the Centenary Test in March, 1977. In the long run, the injury did not affect his bowling, but his throwing arm was never quite the same afterwards.

He could never have been a medium-pacer, partly because it was not in his make-up and partly because, if he had been, somebody would have remodelled his action very early in his career. The justification for Thommo's action was that it enabled him to bowl faster than anyone else around, so nobody was going to say to the young Thomson: 'Look here, son, that's not the way to do it.' However, in my opinion his action lent itself to swinging the ball, but I don't think he was the sort of guy who could have cut his pace and bowled in the same cunning way Dennis Lillee did late in his career. Thommo was born to bowl fast, the faster the better.

Lillee and Thomson will always be mentioned in the same breath, and rightly so, as one of the finest bowling combinations cricket has ever seen. But I don't put Lillee in the naturals category. He did have good natural ability, of course, but I think he is a superb example of someone who became a world champion by working hard at the qualities they had. Dennis, in my opinion, was not an out-and-out natural.

GREG Chappell was. He was certainly one of the most attractive, stylish and technically gifted players ever to play the game. Everything he did looked cultured and caught the eye, the sort of player who looks a million dollars just walking to the crease. It was a natural part of his presence as a player that he should bowl well, far more expertly than he admitted to himself, whether it was medium-pacers or the leg-spin he bowled when he first went into English cricket playing for Somerset. Greg was a fine, clever one-day bowler and a top fielder with wonderfully soft hands. However, it is as an outstanding batsman that he will be remembered. Elegant, unhurried and hitting very straight.

Greg was basically an orthodox player, but, like so many players who perfect the basics, he had the ability to improvise readily when he had to. The limited-overs game was no problem for him, even though he was a classical Test batsman. Most players whose technique is based on orthodoxy can improvise because they have the foundation for a range of strokes. This is a point which is often overlooked when people theorise about how you should play in one-day cricket. Greg had supreme touch and balance, he was the sort of player who never seemed to thrash the ball and yet could hit it many a mile. He was good enough never to need to extend himself, so comprehensively gifted that he always played within the perimeters of his natural style.

No batsman gave me greater watching pleasure than Norman O'Neill. If I could relive an hour watching any man bat, he would be the one. Yet he always played under the added pressure of being a prodigy, of being labelled the 'new Bradman' when he thrilled the crowds early in his career. It was an unnecessary label and a burden Norm could have done without, for he was a magnificent player in his own right. He was talented enough to pitch for Australia at baseball and attract lucrative offers from the United States, and also a very capable leg-spinner who bowled a magnificent wrong 'un and would probably have taken a swag of wickets these days.

He will be remembered, however for his wonderful batting — once seen, never forgotten. He was the classic strokemaking batsman, with a technique straight out of the coaching manual but polished by style and flair that were all his own. If there was a key to his batting it was his uncanny judgment of length. He never seemed to get it wrong and that allowed him to get into position very early and play powerful strokes against deliveries most batsmen would have been happy just to keep out. He was particularly strong on the back foot against fast bowling, capable of bulleting the fastest delivery straight back past the bowler's end stumps before the unfortunate bowler had completed his follow-through. This is a skill enjoyed by few players I have ever seen. Norm developed a reputation as a nervous starter and that was the only flaw in his game, but he thrilled crowds wherever he played. He played 42 Tests, the last in the West Indies in 1965, and scored 2779 runs at a very respectable average of 45.55. But he was the sort of player who did not need statistics to prove his quality. Norm O'Neill was an adventurer and no discussion of the great players should ever leave him out.

HAS anyone ever made batting, bowling and fielding look easier than Mark Waugh? Mark has a touch of genius in everything he does, the sort of player who is always an absolute delight to watch even when you feel he may be squandering a little bit of his talent. Never, never dull. As a fieldsman, Mark has the incalculable advantage of having the softest hands in the business, a cushion which gives with the ball and rarely allows a chance of escape. If he gets a hand on a half chance at slip, he can usually hold the rebound because the ball never bounces far out of his grasp; in the outfield, he has a relaxed body which allows him to adjust even when the ball bounces awkwardly. Even on the roughest outfield, you seldom see him fumble. Mark moves very quickly for a big man, has a strong arm and rarely wastes a second getting rid of the ball. Like his twin, Steve, Mark has lots of sleight-of-hand tricks and when they decide to get competitive it is one of the great delights of the game. He would have made a huge reputation as a first slip and wherever he stands in the cordon he has the old-fashioned virtue of letting the ball come to him rather than offering his hands to the ball. This trait means he can take the ball late and enables him to hold on to chances very wide of his body — and sometimes behind him.

As a bowler, Mark has the versatility to make himself adept at pace or spin. When I first saw him he was a real tearaway with quite a lot of pace. In fact, in his first season in first-class cricket, 1985–86, I had him opening the bowling for NSW, and he could send them down as quickly as anyone in the side. Mark loves to bowl bouncers and will take on any batsman regardless of their reputation. He also has the knack of looking like a lucky bowler — except that I don't think luck has much to do with it. Like Ian Botham at his best, Mark bowls with a lot of imagination and variation and often gets batsmen out with the latest tricky, though often innocuous-looking delivery.

Lately, Mark has struggled against a niggling back injury, but he also spotted a gap in the structure of the Australian side when we went into matches with only Shane Warne as a spinner. Consequently, he turned his hand to bowling off-spin in 1995–96, another skill he has always had in his armoury. When I first saw him bowl offies in the nets I was struck with the naturalness of his style and the easy way he flighted and looped the ball. It is not simply that he can bowl different styles but that he can bowl them so well; I'm sure that if he had been a less-accomplished batsman he could have made an international career out of his bowling and fielding skills. Considering his batting is world class, this adds up to an amazing package.

Unlike his brother, Mark was not rushed onto the international scene. Instead, he made good use of the opportunity to polish his game so that he was equipped for the challenge of Test cricket when it came. Steve Waugh, a bit like Ian Healy, had to learn a lot about cricket while actually playing at Test level and that is very tough. The selectors never doubted Mark's cricket destiny, but some felt he lacked consistency and was prone to get out to soft shots. That was probably true (and sometimes still is) but there comes a time when you have to go along with sheer ability and Mark, like Dougie Walters before him, is one of those rare players who can win a match off his own bat.

By the end of the 1995–96 Australian season, Mark was averaging a respectable 40-plus in Test cricket. I suspect that will still be his average at the end of his career, because he will always have a tendency to frustrate his admirers as well as delight and entertain them. I do not see him as a huge records man, but I do see him as a match winner; they are few and far between and they deserve a bit of special consideration. When Mark enjoys and expresses himself it is as though the game has gone into slow motion — nothing ruffles or hurries him. He is the longest hitter in the side and manages to play his biggest shots with the mark of Mark. When he savages the ball over the top and out of sight, he does it with style.

Mark's style is easy and pleasing to the eye, so much so that it often looks as though he has been dismissed in a 'matter-of-fact' way. There are those ready to claim he lacks Steve's killer instinct or the concentration necessary to be successful, but I don't believe it. They both have enormous ambition to do well in the game, but express it differently. Steve's ambition might have a more public face, but Mark's is just as strong.

FRUSTRATING, exciting, reliable, unreliable, unpredictable, selfish, unselfish, a mug lair, a team player. How many other ways are there of describing one man? And which is the real Dean Jones? I sometimes wonder if we will ever know and perhaps that is the real charm of the bloke.

Deano polarised opinions, people tended to either love or hate him. At one moment he was generous, kind, the first person to offer help to anyone in trouble; at another he was arrogant, mischievously opinionated, prone to flashiness, the flashier the better. The whole man came through into his cricket and that is why he was such an exciting player. In the end, he was just Deano being himself, a mixture of so many traits and qualities. And make no mistake, Dean Jones was one of the finest international batsmen of the modern era. If you doubt it, look at his record.

Deano ranks among the top two or three one-day batsmen the sport has produced. He had everything the one-day batsman needs. He was a complete strokemaker, a great improviser, a magnificently quick runner between the wickets, and a man with total confidence in his own talents who could adjust and tailor an innings to the needs of the situation. At his best he was quite orthodox, especially early in an innings when he hit the bad ball and kept the scoreboard ticking along by knocking better deliveries through the gaps and running like the wind. Nobody in the game has ever turned quicker at the end of a run and he was a peerless judge of what was on. As soon as he played the ball, Deano knew it was one or two or a totally audacious three.

He must have been an absolute nightmare for fieldsmen and he intimidated bowlers who thought they had the measure of most batsmen and then came upon a bloke who enjoyed defying conventions and taking them on. Amid the crowd-pleasing helter-skelter Deano was a very controlled cricketer with a cool brain who did not rely on hitting the skin off the ball. He could do that when he wanted, but his strength was his ability to steer the ball wide or short of fieldsmen and pressure them with the speed of his running. He like to look cocky and arrogant; he usually was. However, he worked within the team plan and a framework he knew he could reproduce like no other batsman around.

The finest one-day innings I have ever seen was played by Dean Jones in Auckland in 1990, when the Australian team was approaching its peak in limited overs and he was very much a key player. He took the great Richard Hadlee to pieces — goading him, charging him and smashing four huge sixes off him on his way to an unbeaten 101. Hadlee was a superb bowler but Jones that day made him look innocuous. There was only one star on the field and that was the batsman with his nose in the air and his head in the clouds. He loved every minute of it and so did we. Everything fell into place — the class and the cheek, the cockiness and the culture, the mental superiority which allowed him to charge and then change his mind and play a dismissive defensive shot on the run. This was Dean Jones to remember.

Later in his career he tended to go over the top, trying to play the impossible shot when it really wasn't on or even necessary. His range of shots was wide enough and tested enough, but he began to go outside it as though he felt compelled to do something different, something only he would attempt. He discovered new ways of getting out and the best batsman in the world is no good in the pavilion. It was the end of a great adventure. Dean Jones made a huge contribution to Australian cricket, both in the Test arena, where his double hundred in the Tied Test in Madras will always be part of the folklore of the game, and in an important one-day culture, where he never failed to entertain. He was a bit bigger than life and why not; he was good for Australia and good for cricket. He helped Australia back to the top of the pile and nobody has ever worn the baggy green cap with greater pride.

I want to end this chapter by looking at a bowler whose career represents what I consider to be one of the biggest tragedies of the 43 years that I've been involved in the first-class game.

Everybody looks back and says, 'If only'. . . and my biggest 'If only' is Bruce Reid. If he had stayed fit, there is no doubt at all that Australia would have been recognised as world champions two or three years before we were able to claim that position simply because he was a great bowler, one of the finest bowlers I have ever seen. None of them reached the crease and delivered the ball as he did, without any apparent effort. He was pure silk. That is what made his injuries all the more surprising; there was nothing in his action to suggest he would put undue strain on his body, far from it. There again, there wasn't a lot of spare muscle on him either.

Bruce was always going to be a class bowler, but in his early days he tended to bowl a metre too short. That earned him a reputation as an unlucky bowler because batsmen played and missed so often against him, but I am always suspicious when that happens. The bowler who consistently beats the batsman without getting an edge is probably not bowling as thoughtfully as he should — you almost invariably find he is bowling too short. Bruce was. When his arm ball cut off the seam, it moved too far for batsmen to get an edge, but they fenced at him. When it happened three or four times an over, the casual spectator reckoned Bruce Reid was the unluckiest bowler around.

Another consequence of bowling too short, of course, was that it gave the ball no time to swing. Bruce became a much better bowler when he pitched the ball up and by the time we toured Pakistan in 1988 he was superb, having apparently overcome a string of injury problems. Alas, he suffered another setback during the third Test in Lahore and faced another series of operations. Ironically, the Australian public probably never saw Reid at his best because the series in Pakistan was not televised, except on the news when the players took strong exception to unfair treatment in the first Test! Those who saw Reid take 14 wickets in the three-Test series knew we were looking at real quality and a wonderful force in Australia's cricket future.

Then Bruce felt a twinge in Lahore, left the field and began a series of battles against injury which eventually defeated him. If Australia had taken their catches on that series, Reid would probably have double his tally of wickets but we had an appalling run and he suffered as much as any of the bowlers. I sometimes wonder if the Australian public realise just what they lost when Bruce was lost to the international game. He was exceptional.

In his early days he had a pretty low level of satisfaction. He was a laid-back sort of character and he tended to be content with three or four wickets in an innings, in fact, it took some time before he took five. That was noticed and the criticism became a little more audible with every match. Good bowler, yeh, but when is he going to get a five-for? I think it niggled him because he began to set his own sights higher, demand more from himself. When Bruce hit his straps he developed a great strike rate; even though his injuries set him back, he made a big impact in the matches he was able to play.

It was a cruel reality of his career that he had more time than most to sit and ponder his future. He was always receptive to advice, in fact nobody was keener than he was to get his body in order and get on with the game. But one injury followed another, often unrelated, which is a medical man's nightmare. He worked hard at all the remedial plans, all the strengthening exercises which they cooked up for him but in the end, perhaps he was just too frail. When we toured the Caribbean in 1991, there was a considerable amount of air travel involved around the islands and Bruce found it almost impossible to sit comfortably in aircraft seats which were a bit restrictive even for those who weren't seven feet tall. His back started to give trouble again and, serious or not, it obviously worried him; the sort of nagging problem any professional sports person can do without.

It was all the more frustrating and eventually all the sadder because, for a very tall bloke with long legs, Bruce was never cumbersome and awkward. Admittedly he wasn't greased lightening in the outfield but he was pretty quick in a straight line and there was a naturalness about his loping stride. The factor which was going to make him a great Test bowler was that he could bowl on any wicket. The nature of the pitch mattered very little because he had the ability to put the ball on the spot, swing it in, take it away. He had a good slower ball… he had everything. If he had stayed fit, he would have notched up over 300 Test wickets. Watching him in action was like watching Mark Waugh batting in full cry. Everything looked easy, inevitable.

CHAPTER 5

Mind games

C ricket is a game in which intelligence and attitude play a vital part. It is very much a mental as well as a physical battle, which is probably why it holds such a fascination for so many people. The skills are sometimes obvious, but the mental joust involved is just as important, arguably more so. Generations of cricketers have played mind games, not only in terms of outwitting the opposition, but also in terms of getting the best out of themselves. There are few games which demand cricket's balance of physical and mental sharpness; the rapid co-ordination of senses with the brain. When a batsman faces a bowler, what you see is rarely what you get.

Modern players, for instance, will talk about judging the 'shape' of a delivery. In the 'old' days, we would have talked about 'assessing the movement', but it all amounts to the same thing. The fact is that when the ball leaves a bowler's hand, it does not always travel in a straight line towards the batsman. There is often an element of flight, even from the fastest bowlers. Michael Holding was greased lightening but he still bowled with flight. And flight adds a difficult dimension for the batsman.

Not all bowlers have it and some disguise it better than others. In fact, it is significant that the best bowlers perfect an action which gives very little away about the delivery they intend to bowl. If the bowler's trajectory is flat, it is easier to judge the length of the ball. The more flight, the more problematic the length and as we have said, judging length is the basis of good batsmanship.

A bowler like Gordon Rorke, the NSW and Australian fast bowler of the late 1950s and early '60s, bowled very fast with an unusual action, but I always found it easy to pick him up. Sure, I found him awkward to play against, but it was not difficult to judge his length because he was a 'flat' bowler. South Africa's leading quick of the '90s, Allan Donald, tends to fall into the same category — several batsmen have told me that he's not that difficult to pick up even though, of course, he is very quick.

For many observers, there tends to be a preoccupation with sheer pace because it represents drama and danger. It may be a little overdone, but I would never underestimate the physical and mental courage which a batsman needs in the face of real fast bowling. The batsman who lacks courage lacks confidence, and will not be able to concentrate on the tell-tale signs at delivery. There is no doubt that a bloke like Charlie Griffith, still regarded by many as the most dangerous fast bowler the West Indies have ever produced, owed a lot to his unpredictability. The bottom line in facing him, however, was courage. My own nemesis was a South Australian, Peter Trethewey, who had only to run up and bowl to have me in all sorts of trouble; I simply could not pick his line and length. Trethewey was nowhere near the fastest bowler I faced, although the record shows that he and his opening partner Alan Hitchcox were both more than a little suspect when it came to the 'purity' of their bowling actions. There was something in Trethewey's delivery I could not fathom, at a time when other blokes were smashing him round the field. All this proves that there are obviously many dimensions to facing fast bowling — timing, reflexes, concentration. But courage is the first requirement and without it nobody plays the fast men well.

Anybody who says he actually likes facing the fast stuff is mad or lying. There is a great sense of achievement and satisfaction at the end of the day when you've come though and done well, but who in his right mind would actually claim to enjoy standing in front of a bloke bowling at 90 miles an hour! The superb West Indian opening bat of the 1950s, Roy Marshall, had a theory that there were two breeds of madman playing cricket: the fast bowler, because he spent his life tearing 30 yards to bowl his guts out, probably on a flat pitch... and the opening batsman, because only a madman would face a madman! Roy probably got it right.

I have no reason to believe that modern batsmen have more courage against fast bowling than players of the past. They wear more protection so they are entitled to look a bit braver, but I reckon that protective cladding can positively work against batsmen, especially when it becomes a substitute for technique. Helmets and padding are there to protect against serious injury, not to make a batsman feel invulnerable. There is a temptation to neglect evasive techniques and rely on the armour plating to absorb every hit; batsmen often take their eyes off the ball, turn their head and let the ball hit them in the knowledge that they will suffer no serious damage. All well and good as far as it goes, yet good batsmen wearing all the protection available have still been badly injured.

However, being hit still hurts and letting yourself be hit is an admission that your defensive technique is lacking. Eventually it saps confidence and when that goes, especially against fast bowling, everything goes with it.

More players get hit by fast bowlers today and that has to be partly because the instinct of self-preservation was a lot stronger when there was no padding to cushion the blow. Players learned evasive techniques because they had to and everybody had his own way of trying to stay out of trouble. I believed it was best to stay in line and duck or weave than just to drop your head and stoop when the ball was dropped short. I was criticised for swaying away occasionally, but when I did I felt balanced and capable of evading the ball. The important thing is to keep your eye on the ball as long and often as possible, and that is particularly important if the bowling is top quality. The very quick West Indian, Andy Roberts, for instance, bowled two bouncers... one distinctly slower than the other. There wasn't much hint from his action which was which so length alone was no guide to how high or quickly the ball would bounce. If you ignored the path of the ball, you were as likely to stoop into it as under it.

They say you never see the punch that knocks you out because, if you were watching, you'd get out of the way. Even if it is just a fraction, perhaps, just enough to deflect the blow or take it on the shoulder. The instincts of self-preservation take over and instinct is quicker than training. Some players set out their stall to hook, some decide to avoid the danger. The important factor is keeping your eyes on the ball and fewer players now seem capable of moving inside or outside the line. They duck without looking or they flinch and let themselves be hit. It is poor strategy because it doesn't stop with the delivery that hurts, whatever batsmen may say. You can see it gradually eating into their confidence — that is what the bowler means it to do, after all — to the point where they are not watching the ball out of the hand. They look for the bouncer, they begin to watch the ball off the pitch and by then it is far too late. Psychologically, the bowler is in charge.

We've had a couple of interesting case histories against the West Indies and I suppose the most obvious is Steve Waugh. He had plenty of courage and determination against the short stuff, but he did not handle it well. This flaw became obvious, and the Windies bowlers, naturally enough, let him have even more. Steve was turning his head away but still going through with shots. We convinced him that he must watch the ball out of the hand rather than try to manufacture something after it pitched. Waiting for the ball to pitch cost him important yards when he could have been picking up the line and moving into position to counter it. He worked hard at it and it's not a crucial weakness now.

Steve still has a healthy fear factor and there is nothing wrong with that. What he has come to terms with is that style isn't everything. Steve once thought it was macho to try and play shots, now he is more pragmatic. He doesn't always look comfortable, but so what? Short-pitched bowling doesn't get him out as often as it did and that is the important thing. He still gets into trouble from time to time, turning his head or riding the delivery which bounces too high to ride, but most of the time he gets inside the line and negotiates the short stuff safely.

When he was in trouble Steve was a good example of the player who watches the ball off the pitch, rarely giving himself enough time to turn his body so he could let the ball go. He ended up with his feet facing towards point and it is well-nigh impossible to turn the ball away safely to the on side from that position. Consequently, he was often caught down the leg side. Now he opens up and lets the ball come on another metre, so that he has more time to get into position. He has loosened his grip a little, too, which helps him to let the ball down softly. Watching the ball more closely and opening his body a bit allows him to work the ball more easily if it is pitched middle stump — and get off strike! Never underestimate the value of turning the strike over and never make the mistake of thinking it shows lack of courage… Good batsmen do not allow themselves to stand in the firing line ball after ball, they work the singles and avoid the cumulative effect of six missiles an over. Fast bowlers rely a great deal on the wearing-down process to force players into the error that gets them out; if batsmen rotate the strike the pressure is halved.

Steve is a very good example of how even the best player can have a problem and work his way through it. None of us likes fast bowling and Steve probably showed that more than most; it became an annoyance and an embarrassment to him. However, he confronted it very professionally, analysed the problem and worked at solving it. The batsman who hooks unselectively or backs away and flashes the bat encourages the bowler; the one who lets the more threatening short stuff go frustrates him. Eventually the bowler has to concede he is burning a lot of energy for nothing. The batsman wins the mind game.

Some players obviously react to the short stuff better than others and it is asking a lot to expect non-batsmen to handle it well. The days when the fast bowlers' union stopped short of bouncing fellow members has long gone so everybody seems to be fair game. The important thing is that all players hit on a method which works for them and stick to it. Take the example of Craig McDermott, who came in for some pretty rough treatment on the 1991 Australian tour to the Caribbean; because of his excellent fast-bowling form he was obviously regarded as a danger man by the Windies and they were determined to soften him up. From the jump, he was bounced and verballed unmercifully, in a plan that was unveiled as early as the second tour match, when Courtney Walsh, next to Curtly Ambrose the best quick in the Caribbean, was allowed to bowl bouncer after bouncer. One speared through the grille of Craig's helmet and hit him above the right eye, a deep and nasty wound which required nine stitches. Yet, McDermott responded splendidly under extreme pressure against the Windies quicks in future encounters — remember the magnificent fourth Test in Adelaide in 1992–93, when he and Tim May put on a thrilling 40 runs for the last wicket and went within one run of an extraordinary victory. Craig knows he will be given the treatment and has worked on his own way of handling it. In many ways he is just like Australian pace bowling colleague, Paul Reiffel, who used to be worried by fast bowling, but now plays the short ball with as much ease as most batsmen — simply because he has decided on the method that suits him.

Adaptation is vitally important. Working out what you have to do and how best to do it is a fundamental part of the mind games of cricket. Circumstances alter, you get older, the opposition varies, your own role in the team changes. Suiting your tactics to the situation is as much a part of playing an innings as footwork and concentration. And it can be learned.

As a young batsman I was a real goer. Anything within reach and I'd whack it. A big driver and a big hooker of the ball… and then I decided I wanted to be an opening batsman. There is a school of thought, of course, that says I should have carried on playing my natural game, happy hooking and all. This sounds fine, but it doesn't always translate into results. As an opening batsman, I decided that I was not going to hook. If the ball was there to be hooked I would just help it on, without ever trying to hit it hard. We had a lot of leg slips in those days so hooking was an extra-risk shot; I had played it well and productively, but I gave it away in favour of a safer stroke which, played carefully, could be quite productive without creating the same risk. It took me a long time to curb my natural instinct to hook, but I worked at it and eventually would have sworn I had revamped my style for good.

When I retired (first time round) in 1968, I had played 52 Test matches and, at 32, was old enough and ugly enough to know my own mind. I continued to play club cricket with Western Suburbs in Sydney, and enjoyed the relaxed atmosphere. And, within half a season, I was hooking again! I was opening the batting against a bloke who had a bit of steam and almost without realising it I found myself going for the big hook-shot. 'You idiot,' I screamed to myself, 'You'll get yourself killed!' But it was a bit late by then. All the training and discipline I had developed to cope with fast bowling went out of the window as soon as I perceived that the need for it was no longer there. It made me realise, if I had ever doubted it, that good habits can be forgotten. And if they can be forgotten, they can be learned as well.

THE MAJOR DIFFERENCE BETWEEN COACHING ELITE PLAYERS AND MORE MODEST PERFORMERS IS PSYCHOLOGICAL. All the good coaches I have ever known have kept it simple and stuck within the fundamentals, irrespective of their target class. Talk to the best Australian football coaches or to the rugby league master, Jack Gibson, and that message comes over loud and clear. I remember one day listening to Graham Lowe, the successful rugby league coach from New Zealand — although the sports are different, his philosophy is exactly the same as mine. Keep it simple, let the blokes know, stick to fundamentals, don't inhibit natural flair. Coaches carp on fundamentals for the very good reason that a player who has mastered the basics and knows why he does what he does will handle the pressures and make fewer mistakes. Fundamentals don't have to be boring — left elbow up and all that — but they do have to be part of a good player's knowledge of the art of what he is doing.

Players naturally respond differently to being coached. Some accept advice and criticism better than others; some resent it and others lap it up. The one I like least is the bloke who pretends he knows. You get half way through a bit of corrective advice and he butts in: 'Yeh, I know.' Try to elaborate on the point and off he goes again: 'Yeh, I know.' He doesn't know, of course, but he is never going to admit it; his ego won't allow it. So in the end you have to hit him with; 'Well, if you know, what the hell are you doing it for?' He will probably shrug.

Then again, some players are so desperate to absorb advice that they grab every bit that's going, contradictory or not. They are so anxious to learn that they don't really evaluate what they are being told. Justin Langer is a young batsman with a huge amount of ability, but he is one of those who tries to practise everything everybody else preaches; he listens to so many people he becomes confused. I advised Justin that at his career stage he has to differentiate between listening to advice and trying to put it all into some sort of complete-cricketer formula. Be selective. Listen to advice, by all means, but don't adopt it unless it's really worthwhile.

The super-talented player needs careful handling because nobody, least of all a coach, wants to inhibit his natural flair. I don't believe, however, that natural talent will take a young player all the way in professional sport. A very small minority may make their own way to the top, but not many. Only a handful out of millions treading the path will succeed in this way. I tell players that most of what they achieve up to the age of 17 or so has more to do with genetics than genius; their parents probably deserve the credit for getting the mix right. They grin sheepishly, but I reckon they take the point. You only have to look at the number of brilliant-looking youngsters in all sports who burn out and never achieve despite their very high potential. In most cases, they had the talent but never learned the nuts and bolts of their trade. The how came so easily they never bothered to explore the why. When things go wrong — call it 'loss of form' if you like — they do not have the basics to fall back on.

As a young sportsman I was a bit of a hotshot. Name any ball-sport and I was pretty good at it — golf, tennis, baseball whatever. I made the NSW Sheffield Shield team at 16 and I suppose I could have graduated to the Australian side thinking I had it all made. As it turned out, I was dropped for two years and only cemented a place in the side after the great Neil Harvey took me to one side and gave me a bit of advice which was probably the most important of my career. 'You have all the talent, but you've got to think a bit more about what you are going to do,' he said. 'Where do you think you would stand the best chance of getting into the Australian team?' Jimmy Burke, who with Colin McDonald had formed a very effective opening partnership for Australia, had just retired and Australia were having a problem finding a replacement. Going to the top of the batting order suddenly seemed like a good idea, as I knew deep down that at that point in the history of Australian cricket my natural ability was not going to be enough to upstage the established stars in the middle order — men such as Neil, Peter Burge, Norman O'Neill, Les Favell and Ken Mackay. Neil's advice put my thinking back on track. I had to learn a lot and relearn some things I thought I already knew, but it was obvious in my case that ability was not enough on its own to guarantee an international career. It is a lesson even the most naturally-gifted have to bear in mind.

Michael Slater is a good example of the very talented young batsman working to develop an effective approach to the game at the highest level. He ran into trouble with the hook shot on the 1995 West Indies tour and clearly had to work out whether it was a stroke worth the risk in his particular case. He had to decide what he wanted to be. The best hookers I have seen were those with short backlifts and, like Keith Stackpole, compact and powerful men. Ian Chappell liked the stroke, but did not play it well because he was an 'up-and-under' hooker; the shot produced the occasional dramatic six, but never convinced bowlers they couldn't get him out. When we analysed Michael Slater's innings, we found the hook had not played a major and certainly not a particularly productive part. His own feeling and the 'wagon-wheels' of his innings confirmed that. Michael will work out his own methodology, but he is a good avoider of the ball and has enough shots at his disposal without worrying about the hook too much. Why encourage the bowlers and take a risk of getting out?

An experienced batsman can develop a sort of sixth sense about a bowler's intentions. Everything at top level happens in an unbelievably short timescale but it is possible to lock little factors away in the mind's computer and pull them out when they are needed. The key is concentration, which is not the same thing as gazing fixedly at the bowler. Don't worry too much about the first half of his approach; that is going to tell you very little. However, as the bowler nears the bowling crease there may be tell-tale signs of the sort of delivery he intends to bowl. The better the bowler, the fewer the clues, but a successful batsman will train himself to pick up minor differences in a bowler's approach.

Most bowlers who intend to bowl a bouncer need to get the extra impetus from somewhere. They may accelerate slightly, some need to use their body more, others may carry an elbow slightly differently. The early-warning signals may be very small but they have to be registered in the computer. Also, just to confuse matters, they cannot be taken on face value. Because the bowler plays mind games of his own any variation in his approach may be a ploy to deceive you. He has accelerated, but he may intend to bowl a slower ball; he has gone wide of the crease to slant one in, or perhaps he just wants to make you believe that is his intention. Why do some bowlers like to go off a short run and then bowl a bouncer? What you see is not always what you get, but the observation is vital because you then feel you are matching the bowler in the battle of wits. If it sounds very complicated in print, the fact is that batsmen do it naturally with practice. Like tying a shoelace or knotting a tie. The computer eventually stores away each bowler's characteristics and makes them available on demand. However, you must never make a final judgment until the ball leaves the bowler's hand. That is when the bowler makes a decision on the type of delivery and that is when you make yours.

Every bowler has his theories about how he should be able to dismiss a batsman. He studies a batsman's preferences — or at least he should — works out his strengths and weaknesses, and bowls with a plan. A good bowler puts as much preparation into his game as any batsman, so it was my aim as a batsman to make sure that the bowler never got me out in the way he intended. If a bowler got me out as planned, I felt insulted. The best way to counter the bowler's plan is with a plan of your own. Feed every observation into the computer, do as much pre-planning as possible and then you will not have to rely solely on instinct. That is particularly helpful when you face the fastest bowlers because reaction time is so very short. It is, however, just as important if you face a wily, scheming bowler with a mixed bag of tricks. Facing Shane Warne will never be easy, but no decent batsman would go in against him without some sort of appreciation of what he does and how best to counter it. The fact that batsmen are aware of that and he still gets them out is what makes Warne such an exceptional talent.

In Warne's case, a simple game plan would be to play forward to counteract a very dangerous delivery like the flipper. If Warne is looking for a catch, he is likely to bowl middle and leg, trying to persuade the batsman to play across the line and clip a return catch or something to mid-on off a leading edge. If I drive, I'll make sure I drive straight down the ground. No plan is foolproof, as Warne's victims know only too well, but a basic philosophy on how to play any bowler is essential. It need not to followed slavishly and it need not be defensive, however good the bowler might be.

As a batsman, I always wanted to hit the ball for four. That was the basis of my game plan against every bowler. It is easier to come down the scale than aim higher so the approach should be: Can I get a four? Or three? Two then? Okay, I'll settle for a single. If you set out to play an innings concentrating on defence, the chances are you will miss out on relatively easy runs; by the time you realise a delivery was there to be hit, the moment has gone. Trying to switch the game plan from defence to attack in mid-stroke is a sure recipe for disaster. The mental process should be aggressive and I have always believed that taking singles is a very aggressive way of playing the game. Conceding six singles an over is no part of any bowler's plan. This strategy is very much a part of the current Australian team's approach and it has worked wonders in the limited-overs game.

Interestingly, a couple of the Australian players believe we have developed a tendency not to look for twos, to think only in terms of fours or singles. If so, it suggests to me that batsmen are thinking too much about playing the big shot and it could explain why so many players seem to get out when they are set. As far as I am concerned, a batsman who has made 15 runs is set, but there is a fashion in all forms of cricket these days for players not to capitalise on good starts. Perhaps, as in so many things, the key is in the mind games.

We hear a lot of talk these days about being aggressive, but the best players have always been mentally aggressive whether they were batting, bowling or fielding. When I fielded at slip, I willed every ball bowled to come to me. Every one. 'Geez, I hope he doesn't nick it . . .' — the bloke who has that sort of attitude will never be a successful fieldsman and, for sure, will never take many catches. Years ago, I was fielding at first slip and I asked the bloke at third slip if he would swap. I just felt I could take a catch there. Sure enough, first ball after the switch I took a catch — it was the weirdest thing imaginable. Wanting to be involved in the game is vital to playing it well; reflexes are sharper, the adrenalin pumps harder, the brain works overtime. Thinking negatively dulls your senses; the computer switches off.

Top-order batsmen set out their stall to play long innings. It is their job in the framework of a five-day Test match and it takes a particular mental attitude to see it through. It is easy to panic, to watch the scoreboard and be self-critical, to create your own pressures. In a purely practical sense, it is hard to concentrate for every second of what might turn out to be hours in a Test innings. The batsman in the right frame of mind for playing a long innings will make sure he does not waste concentration; he will concentrate totally when it matters and allow himself to relax when it doesn't.

Nobody can achieve what I call peak concentration for the 120 minutes of a two-hour session, let alone a long innings. And peak concentration is what we are looking for. Consequently, the long-innings batsman learns to relax between deliveries, to reduce his peak concentration to the minimum, to keep himself sharp for the moments when his concentration must be white-hot. The notion that a batsman has to concentrate for every second of his innings is one of those truisms which is misleading if you take it literally. There have to be periods of mental relaxation. If you cut down your peak concentration to, say, five seconds a delivery, the mental challenge is tough, but not overwhelming. The secret of batting for a long time is to focus totally when it matters, not to develop a headache applying yourself with a squint to every second of the innings. Stay sharp for when sharpness is needed. With practice, reducing concentration time to the repetitive but crucial few moments becomes routine. You know how to do it, you harness the ability to respond and relax in turn.

But it takes time and the mind has a habit of wanting to race off on its own. Even Test batsmen go through periods when they respond to what they want to happen rather than to what is actually going on. 'I hope this bloke drops short because I know I can cut him.' Or when facing the spinner: 'I reckon I should hit this one back over his head.' Even at the highest level, pre-judging the situation happens a lot more than most batsmen would care to admit. I can vouch for that.

After playing in a solitary Test against the Englishmen in 1958–59 as a middle-order batsman, I was left out of the Australian side for the following season's tour to India and Pakistan. And then, when I came back into the team against the West Indies in 1960–61, as an opening batsman — against Wes Hall of all people in the first Tied Test — I went through one of the most embarrassing experiences of my career. This occurred simply because I pre-judged a delivery from their marvellous spinner, Sonny Ramadhin, and played it for what I wanted it to be rather than for what it actually was.

I had reached 92 and was desperate for my first Test century. And I suddenly found myself trying to sweep the ball from the off stump. I had become so anxious about the century that I convinced myself the ball was around leg stump and ripe for sweeping; I wanted to believe that because I had already fashioned the stroke in my mind. For a few seconds I was prepared to hope the ball would behave as I wanted it to. Simpson, bowled Ramadhin, 92. Serves me right.

It is not difficult to convince yourself that you are concentrating really hard when really you are not thinking logically. Slips fieldsmen need a special sort of concentration but you often see them start to wander, you can spot it a mile off. The ball is nicked and the bloke in the slips jumps as if he's had a terrible fright. Yet he's been staring fixedly at the bat all day. His moment of peak concentration has passed before the batsman got an edge, trying too hard to concentrate simply made it worse. It's a matter of relaxation and training.

Limited-overs cricket is a mental game, of course, and I reckon it's the simplest form of the game. It's only made difficult by those who play it. Most of the rules are framed in favour of a high-scoring game, so all a batsman has to do is take advantage of the restricted field placings and push the ball into the gaps. It sounds very easy, but its an awful game for self-imposed pressures; the bowler does his job and keeps it tight and suddenly the batsman is looking at the scoreboard and fretting. The tension that builds in a batsman who is not scoring runs is quite incredible.

The best way to mentally counter this stress is to know your targets and understand the game plan. That often comes back to the ability of the captain or coach to say: 'This is what we are looking for.' Once a player knows what the tactics are he can put himself in context and probably find the situation a lot less demanding. His role may change with the state of the game; he may need to be careful or highly adventurous, he may even have to sacrifice himself. As long as the team plan is paramount, he should not put pressure on himself by worrying about what others may think.

Human nature being what it is, the theory is often a good deal more comfortable than the practice. Bowlers have a right to bowl maiden overs if they are good enough and all at once the batsman feels distinctly hot under the collar. His palms are sweaty, his timing is off and shots begin to find fieldsmen with unerring accuracy. That builds even more tension. 'Geez, I can't get the ball through the damned field. What's wrong with me? I'm batting like a drunk. I must do something different.' And you see the unmistakable signs of a batsman going beyond what he knows he can do well. The pressure is taking its toll. How often in his life does a Test player try to hit to 'cow-shot corner'? How often will he try it in a limited-overs match under pressure? Few realise it's one of the hardest shots to play, yet experienced players try it because they reckon that is where the gap is. True enough, but the gap is there on purpose, to make the batsman play the way the bowler wants rather than the way he knows he can play. It is part of the trap and if the batsman accepts the risk, it is usually because he has been pressured into thinking he has no alternative.

Some batsmen begin to draw away to leg, making room to whack the ball through the off-side. Improvisation, they say. In fact, what they have decided is where they think the ball will be bowled and in doing so have seriously cramped their options, the areas in which they can hit the shot. Anything on their legs and they are dead ducks. Far better in my book to advance straight to the ball, better to charge and have the option of playing a stroke in different directions. When the pressure is on you have to have faith in your ability, be disciplined, remember what made you successful and don't pre-empt what the bowler is going to do.

Many players, even top-level ones, don't give enough real thought to where they should play shots and why. If a batsman wants to hit the ball in the air, for instance, there is only one place in limited-overs cricket where he should hit it and that's over the heads of the close-in fieldsmen. There is no point in hitting the ball in the air between inner fieldsmen; if the captain and bowler know what they are doing the outfield area in that arc will be covered. If you are going to hit over the top, aim straight over the head of the bowler, point, cover, midwicket… and if you have enough elevation you have a reasonable chance of getting away with a mishit. Too often batsmen are caught on the boundary by fieldsmen who don't have to move. Where was that shot supposed to be going? A player like Glenn Turner became a genius at the one-day game because he never exhausted himself or dislocated anything trying to carry the boundary; he chipped the ball over the infielders' heads into the gaps beyond. When he didn't quite connect properly, the ball almost invariably fell short of the men in the deep. I don't think he was lucky to get away with the lofted shots, he knew his strengths and weaknesses and he was mentally selective.

Incidentally, I think Australians are traditionally poor hitters over the top. It may be because our grounds are so big, certainly compared with most other countries, so its not really a percentage shot in domestic cricket. A few players live by the belief that 'there's more room in the air', but generally that's a fallacy. If you try and hit a six at the MCG, you had better get it right because the outfielders have all day to get under it if you don't. The Indians are brilliant big-hitters. Little blokes, often quite frail-looking, can hit the ball huge distances. The biggest six I have ever seen was at Bangalore in India, during the opening game of our tour there in 1986. The ground there is a huge stadium, built on the lines of the MCG with a double-decker stand. Our left-arm spinner, Ray Bright, was bowling and their wicketkeeper, Sadanand Viswanath, who must weigh all of 57kg, unleashed a six which has probably not returned to earth yet. And this was 10 years ago. Ray's first reaction was to shout: 'Catch it!' Then he watched with his mouth open as the ball disappeared over the scoreboard and the stand; it was still going up when it disappeared from sight. The West Indies are pretty powerful hitters, the English are not big hitters over the top in

Australia because they are used to smaller grounds and they know they will struggle if they try to hit sixes. However, the Indians certainly lead the field in weight-for-effect big hitting and I have never fully understood why.

But I must emphasise that one-day cricket isn't a sloggers game. The most successful players work it out and play the percentages just as they would in first-class cricket or Tests. The same basic techniques and careful mental approach apply, and it is something of a truism that the best players are effective at both.

Part of the mind game of cricket is knowing how to cope with being out of form, or luck, or touch or whatever the struggling player wants to call it. A basic rule for the player who suddenly finds himself in a slump is not to put himself under unnecessary pressure. Work the ball around, get off strike. That is not being selfish, it is simply being sensible. An innings of 50 singles will help form better than one of four fours. What we call form is basically a frame of mind; you do not lose your ability overnight or even from one match to another. Your degrees of perfection will change but your ability is always there waiting to be tapped.

A player with the right attitude can get runs even when he is out of form and some players have been particularly good at this. David Boon is a good example of the sort of player who can play substantial innings even when he is not in top form — and his attitude towards the job is legendary. England do not have a player in that mould and that is one reason why they have struggled in recent years. English batsmen generally strike the ball better than Australians, they are wonderful timers of the ball, but they have been lacking players who respond strongly under real pressure. It seems as though every batsman has to be in top form before he can play a major innings. That must come down to poor selection; it is hard to believe that there are no alternatives. A bloke like David Steele, who had scored some runs against Australia and the West Indies in the mid 1970s, was able to come into the side and do well in a particular situation and there must still be players like him in the county game. Unless, of course, the mental set-up is all wrong. When I was recalled to Test cricket in 1977, I definitely found the mental side of things tougher to re-train than the physical. It was remarkable how many of the younger players found it so hard to concentrate for long periods yet they were half my age. However, I had been through it before, so, because I was mentally tougher, I was going harder than they were at the end of the day.

Everybody who plays Test cricket is a very good player, so there has to be something which sets the really top ones apart and I'm convinced that a lot of it is mental. Nous is a good old-fashioned word for what the successful players share. Their styles may vary, but they all have an instinct for staying at the crease, picking the gaps, creating big innings. When you look at batsmen such as Graeme Pollock or Gary Sobers or Brian Lara you see men who rarely hit the ball to fieldsmen. They know how to transfer pressure from themselves to the bowlers. There again, the best bowlers have nous and the ability to work batsmen out, to analyse a batsman's style and the ability to exploit a weakness. Australia's success on the 1995 West Indies tour was built around a lot of planning and team discussion; in all my years I have never seen a team bowl better to plan. So often the best-laid plans fall apart because the bowlers don't have the mental toughness to stick to the pattern, but there was never a sign of that in the Caribbean. Lara scored his 50s, but he made too many mistakes on the way; our bowlers stuck to the game-plan and we invariably got him out in a way we had discussed.

Successful players are often described as arrogant and there is often a lot of truth in that. However, it is the arrogance developed by a cricketer who knows how to handle the situation, who feels confident in his ability to survive and dominate. A state player once commented on the fact that I looked as though I was just coming to the office every day, confident, in control. 'Well I'm a Test cricketer,' I said. 'I should have things well under control in a Shield match shouldn't I?' Arrogant, perhaps. Cocky. I can't deny that I felt in control of the situations, I had confidence in my ability. That's why a bowler with nous strives to take a batsman into areas he is not comfortable with, to loosen his control and outsmart him. A lot of factors come into play, including ability, confidence which dispels fear of failure, experience and attitude. The ones who play the mind games best are the ones who succeed.

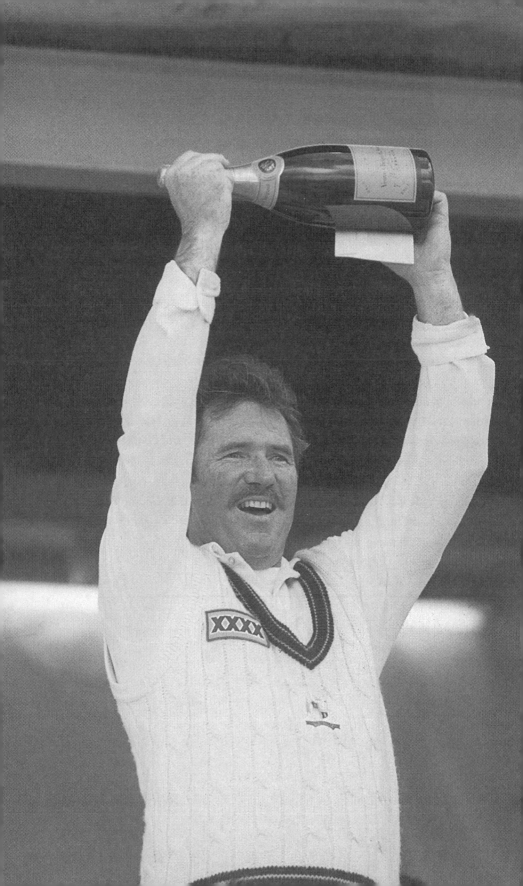

CHAPTER 6

AB & other self-made men

They called him 'Captain Grumpy' and worse. He could be a difficult sort of character which only made him all the more interesting. And Allan Border was the finest captain of international one-day cricket I have ever seen.

Allan's contribution to Australian cricket is hard to over emphasise when you contrast the state it was in when he became captain with the healthy situation he left behind. Some say he went on a little too long and I cannot argue with that, but a lot of players have been prone to the same thing over the years and it certainly should not overshadow the valuation of an extraordinary career. AB took over the side in 1983–84 when it was at a desperately low ebb, applied himself hard to a job he did not really want, and had an enormous influence on the revival of the team. It is worth emphasising that when he became captain, there was nobody else around who could do the job in the way that it needed doing. Nobody. It is a debatable point whether his character moulded the team or the situation at the time moulded his approach, but it is a fact that he never quite lost the touch of pessimism which he learned early in his captaincy years. Perhaps he could never quite convince himself that the wheels would not fall off and that detracted a bit from his status as a Test match captain. However, in the limited-overs game he had no equal. He developed a feel for one-day cricket which was quite extraordinary.

The image of AB as a touchy sort of bloke passed into legend and he certainly was not all sweetness and light, not that there was any reason why he should be. Australia needed a bloke who would lead them, man the trenches, create an attitude — not somebody who was good at making speeches and soft as putty on the field. His great strength was his cussedness and his great weakness, perhaps, was his dislike of confrontation. A lot of players who deserved it have winced under a withering glare from AB, but not too many can claim to have copped a real volley from the captain. When he was angry or dissatisfied he tended to withdraw rather than square up to the problem. So he could be moody but he was never really unpredictable.

A lot of people liked to describe him as complicated but I never found him that way; I thought he was a straightforward bloke who had his off days like the rest of us. Let's face it, cricket-wise he did not have a great deal to be cheery about in his early years as captain. He carried a huge burden and sometimes must have felt that it was AB versus the world. He was focused on cricket, perhaps even blinkered. He liked nothing better than to play for a day then prop himself at a bar for a while with a few mates, probably talking about cricket. He had very strong principles about how the game should be played, a well-publicised affection for Test cricket as the superior form of the game; he was the first bloke to call a batsman back if a catch was not taken cleanly, that sort of thing. Yet he could get into the umpires if he thought they had made a mistake, and stand his ground with the single-mindedness which came through in his batting.

Allan did have a tendency to bottle things up within himself and let small annoyances become mini-crises before he tackled them. That was part of his dislike of confrontation. When AB was in a bad mood the thunderclouds gathered, bit by bit, and a slight wisp of steam from the ears slowly became a steady stream until suddenly he'd snap. Probably about something he could have solved with a quiet word an hour earlier. Five minutes later and he would have forgotten about it.

We never had an argument the whole of the time we worked together. He could be contrary, but it never came to a stand-up fight or a slanging match. I think that derived from a great deal of mutual respect; I had played club cricket against him, helped him out with a bit of promotional work when he was 18. And we knew that we were both heading in the same direction. I also believe AB needed me — and also the media manager Ian McDonald and physio Errol Alcott — and was honest enough to admit it. He did not really like the peripherals that go with being Australia's captain — the media involvement, the need to organise practice and so on — and he was happy to delegate to blokes who were there for that purpose. AB liked to play, simple as that. He didn't mind hard work at training and practice, although he admitted it got no easier. However, he was the sort of bloke who liked to participate rather than organise. What evolved was a system which, whatever the critics may say, lifted the profile of Australian cricket.

As a batsman AB has my total respect. He was a made cricketer, a player with a fair amount of talent who then turned himself a world-class player through determination and cussedness. He had a great awareness of the extent of his own abilities, knew just what he was capable of except in the vexed area of bowling. He never did enough of that. He became the man for the crisis, the bloke who would bat on when others failed, the one who never gave himself away. It was a necessary quality in the early years because the side was pretty weak and, looking back, it must have taken a lot out of him. It certainly took character to carry the burden when there was very little light at the end of the tunnel and a lot of lesser men would have cracked. There were times as captain when he was frightened to get out because he felt that if he did, the team would collapse. That doesn't do much for your style, but it says a hell of a lot about your attitude. Even towards the end, when the runs became harder to make, you could see the old AB cussedness. He wasn't going to get out, not him. His square cut used to be a favourite and very profitable stroke; he lost it five years ago and that put huge pressure on his ability to score freely, but he just loved playing the game, even when it was tough. We forced him to take a couple of matches off once to rest a hamstring and he was absolutely dirty on the world. It was for his own good, of course, and he acknowledged that later on, but at the time he simply could not come to terms with not actually playing the game.

I think he underestimated himself badly as a bowler because he proved time and time again that he had the ability to take wickets and that's what bowling is all about. However, trying to persuade him to bowl was sheer horsework. I recall a Test match against Sri Lanka in Hobart; there was a partnership on, the pitch was beginning to turn and we were a bit short of bowlers. Just the situation for AB to have a go. At lunch I suggested that was the way to go. Add a bit of variety, this is your sort of pitch, you're the man for the job. He appeared quite enthused. I reminded him twice before the players went out and he was adamant. 'No worries, I'll do it,' he said as he walked onto the field. He did not bowl a ball in the match. 'I thought about it and the others bowlers were better than me,' he commented later. I remember another time, at Edgbaston in Birmingham during the 1985 Ashes tour, when he announced in despair that he was probably Australia's best bowler. It was as though that was the worst thing he could think of to say. Perhaps that was the clue to his reluctance as a bowler — a lack of self-esteem and an unwillingness to make his bowlers feel that using himself reflected on their ability. A shame.

Given his reputation as the stalwart saviour of the side as a batsman, it would be wrong to underestimate the flair and instinct which Allan had for the game. It came out in his one-day captaincy and in his fielding, which was often just brilliant. He did not have an exceptionally strong arm but he hit the stumps when he had to more often than anybody — the secret to this was his ability to read the play and position his feet before the ball arrived. He did not appear to move that quickly, but he did not have to because his positioning was intuitive. Some fieldsmen look spectacular as they descend on the ball at a million miles an hour and take two metres to deliver it while the batsman saunters home. AB just nailed 'em.

Allan had a highly-developed cricket brain, which is not surprising when you remember that he was so wrapped up in the game and loved nothing more than to talk about it. He had a great instinct for the right moment and the mental toughness to back his judgment. Watching closely over the years, I was enthralled at AB's ability to make bowling changes at just the right time, particularly in one-day matches. A bowler might be taking some stick and you'd think it was time to make a change, but AB would hang on for an over, maybe two or three, and a wicket would fall. And when he did bring on a new bowler, that man usually took a wicket early on. It was a fine instinct and no captain in the world had more of it.

It is easy to be an adventurous captain when you have the world's best bowling attack behind you, when you can throw up the ball and wait for Lillee or Thommo or one of half a dozen West Indians to grab it and bowl you to victory. Allan Border never had the luxury of a ready-made team of winners and that fact clearly shaped the nature of his captaincy. The game was not always as joyful and carefree as he would have liked it to be. He was, however, an absolutely essential factor in the revival which Australian cricket enjoys now, a player and a captain who deserves a special place in the Australian game.

MOST sports people, even those who make it to the very top, rely on a hell of a lot of hard work and application to get the most out of their ability. They are not quite naturals but they are outstanding in their willingness to put in the hours it takes to make it to the top and then stay there. They make the most of whatever talent they have been given and many become truly outstanding players.

'Smell it out,' they used to say. 'Keep your head over the ball, concentrate hard, minimise mistakes.' I have no doubt that Bill Lawry read that somewhere as a young man and made it the watchword of a very fine career. Okay, so Bill had more equipment than most for the smelling out business... but my word how he got his head down for Australia in many hours of need, in a Test career that began on the 1961 Ashes tour of England and ended in controversial circumstances when he was dropped, as captain and as a team member, for the final Test of the 1970–71 Ashes series in Australia. In his own way, the 'Phantom', as he was known, was a great player, a classic example of a cricketer achieving great things through professional application.

Bill did not lay claim to much God-given talent. However, he had guts, determination and, even though it was often underestimated, a very sharp and clever cricket brain. Distant observers reckoned he must be a dour sort of individual, uninteresting and not really passionate about the game. Have you heard him commentate? Bill is a witty, bright man to be with, a great practical joker and a bloke who has a droll line for any situation.

He did not have enough natural talent, however, to be able to spread it thin. He could not play to the gallery or project himself to the public, instead he needed to direct all his concentration to batting for a living. Bill's gifts stopped well short of being a song and dance man; he could not allow an ounce of his ability to be diverted from the job of doing his best out in the middle. Yet, he was so focused that he became a great player of his type — in his time, the most difficult Test batsman in the world to dislodge. That is not a distinction which professionals of any era take lightly.

Phanto built his game around the simplest possible fundamentals. His style was set in concrete. In his early days he was quite a formidable hooker, but he eventually reckoned it was not a percentage stroke for the opening batsman with responsibilities measured in hours and he gave it away. He was a maddeningly slick runner between wickets, which highlighted a real skill in placing the ball, and, as a bloke who has always preached the value of taking singles, I found our styles blended. In terms of rotating the strike and keeping the scoreboard ticking over without needing to smash fours and sixes, we were possibly the most aggravating partnership in cricket; I'd like to think so.

Phanto was also tough, mentally and physically. I remember the 1965 tour of the Caribbean, when we copped a fair bit of stick from Wes Hall and Charlie Griffith before we put on 382 for the first wicket in the fourth Test, in Barbados. There was no numerical restriction on bouncers in those days and, since it was the first season experimenting with the front-foot bowling rule, the West Indian umpires tended to be a bit liberal in their definition of no-balls. There was, as they say, a fair bit of leeway. We copped a barrage of short stuff during our partnership and then, in the second innings, Bill was hit in the face by a nasty delivery which reared and flew past his upthrust gloves. The West Indian fieldsmen gathered round, asking if he was okay and the like, but Bill gestured them away. 'You've been trying to knock our heads off all series, so what's it to you?' he roared. 'Buzz off, the lot of you.' Undiplomatic, perhaps, but as forthright as Bill himself. I don't know how many times I watched Phanto from 22 yards away, but it was always a great comfort to have him there on your side.

There is a fairly modern theory that to be successful on the field, it is necessary to spend a lot of time together off it. That has worked for some partnerships. The case of Geoff Marsh and David Boon springs immediately to mind — they were great mates, pretty well inseparable off the field, and it appeared to make them all the more effective at the office. However, Bill and I were individuals with quite different off-field pursuits — I'm not sure I'd know one end of a pigeon from the other — and we certainly did not live in each other's pockets. A meal together from time to time was about it. But on the field we had enormous respect and affinity for each other. If I was in trouble he'd try to get me off strike and viceversa; I was a more competent player of spin bowling than Bill and I'd try to exploit it; we both ran each other's singles. Simple, professional attitudes. We used to say we worked on the principle that, as opening batsmen, the best place to be was at the bowler's end. It worked pretty well.

Bill still tells the story about us facing Hall and Griffith for the first time on that '65 tour, in the first Test in Jamaica. Simpson asks for an adjustment of the sight-screen. 'Somewhere around middle, please,' he says 'Between me and that bugger, Wes Hall.' Not true, I swear, but a good story. In the lead-up to that series, we had heard a lot about Griffith, but we never faced him until that Test in Jamaica. And there he was, pushing off the sight screen to begin a slow, ambling run. I was facing and had the thought: 'Good, he needs a warm-up ball. I'll get chance to have a look at him.' But then he hit the delivery stride, unwound and crash, my middle stump was flying out of the ground. Fortunately, the umpire was signalling no-ball. And right next to the 'ump' was Bill Lawry, grinning, rolling his eyes and making huge expressive bowling 'gestures' with a very bent arm! That fired up Charlie no end, as you might imagine. And I swear this story *is* true.

As I said, Bill was finally dropped from the Australian side in extraordinary circumstances. There must have been some sort of philosophy behind the decision (Australia were one Test down at the time, with one to play), but I cannot imagine what it was; no player, let alone the captain, should be dropped from the side in that fashion. Whatever criticisms that might have been levelled at him, there was no doubt that he was totally committed to Australia's cause. Victorians still get mighty hot under the collar at the way he was treated and I can't say I blame them. There is no doubt in my mind that if Bill had continued to lead the side which Ian Chappell inherited, he would have been just as ruthless and effective as Ian proved to be.

CRICKET (OR GOLF, TENNIS, BASEBALL, MAHJONG, SNAKES AND LADDERS) IS A SIMPLE GAME MADE DIFFICULT BY COACHES. We've all heard that one often enough and I have even heard coaches arguing which is the most difficult game because that seems to lend it a certain mystique. I'm sure some games are more difficult than others and I'm also sure some games are made more difficult than they need to be. However, I cannot honestly say I regard cricket as a simple game to play well. I think that is basically because of the time factor involved. Cricket shares obvious basics with games like baseball or tennis, but it stands alone in terms of the time a match takes and, within that match, the time a player has to dwell on the next move. The cricketer has time to think — and that does not make the game easier to play.

Concentration is not easy to sustain over a six-hour day at the crease or in the field. In fact, it is well-nigh impossible and the ability to distil concentration into the moments it really matters is vital. That is a skill which can be learned and it is part of a coach's job to look at the mind games as much as the technicalities involved. The ability to relax between deliveries, for instance, has always been associated with effective slips fieldsmen but it applies as much to batsmen and even to bowlers. There are techniques which help but they have to be worked on and practised hard if they are to become second nature. The higher the standard, the more skills are needed and it is one of the ironies of top-level sport that people are deceived by how easy they look. Nobody should assume that cricket is an easy game to play, simply because a Test cricketer makes excellence look commonplace.

That is why I have always had the greatest respect for players who are not blessed with huge talent, but who achieve great standards by their ability to work intelligently hard. No decent coach wants to undermine the naturalness of players or stifle genuine flair, but neither should he accept the superficial as evidence of talent. How often do we see players with a pleasing style given preference over players who turn in the performances but who don't look nearly as polished? It happens a lot more than it should.

In fact, a flowing style can often disguise a multitude of basic problems which will eventually be exposed. That's why the game's history is studded with truly elegant players rather than dominated by them. Such stylists achieve huge public affection, of course, and, cricket being a writers' game, become lionised in purple prose. However, they are the exception rather than the rule. The modern game has not enjoyed many Greg Chappells but it has produced a large number of wonderfully effective players — David Boon, Geoff Marsh and Steve Waugh for instance. You couldn't in all conscience describe them as elegant, even though they have had their moments and played elegant shots. Other infinitely more elegant batsmen have proved much less productive at the top level.

But, boy, don't selectors just love to pick them.

NO discussion of players who made themselves top-class by utilising every bit of their ability could possibly exclude Geoffrey Boycott, a man most Australians (and many Englishmen) love to hate, but one I consider to be one of the most fascinating characters who has ever played the game. There is no doubt that Geoff is a more complete batsman now, from the comfort of the commentators' box, than he ever was as a player. However, nobody should underestimate his ability or the particular qualities which drove him to make himself one of the world's most formidable players. Limited, for sure, but conscious of his capabilities and a master at playing to his strengths.

Back in 1968, when I had retired from the game and Geoff was busy carving out a singular reputation, I wrote that he struck me as a batsman who practised his strokes in front of a mirror — and probably in a very limited space between his bed and the wall! In his early days, his footwork was so severely limited that he was woefully vulnerable outside the off stump. He worked it out with experience, being Boycott he would, but in his first series against Australia, in 1964, he was easy meat for our fast-medium outswing bowler, Grahame Corling, who consistently had him caught at slip. Boycott's stunted footwork meant he could not hope to cover the perimeter. I still have this vision of the young Boycott practising hour after hour in front of a tall, thin mirror with no room to move his feet; I must check the theory out some time.

Geoff was a complex character who sometimes bottled things up until they got on top of him and sometimes opened his mouth a little too wide for his own good. And, although he had his limitations in 1964, he was obviously a player who would go on to make his mark in world cricket. He had the desire about him, even then. But during that series, in an interview which he should have considered more carefully, he admitted that before he went in to bat he liked to sit quietly in a corner and meditate for a few minutes about what lay ahead. Some chance. I immediately delegated our 12th man to make sure he had at least a dozen autograph books ready for Boycott's signature when he was getting ready to go out and bat. Geoff probably wondered how it was that the Australians took such an interest in him at such an inconvenient time. But that's the way it is in top-class sport: if somebody gives you half a chance you take advantage of them. Boycott learned that quickly enough.

Geoff soon worked out all the angles. His great success was built chiefly on the fact that he made himself a technically good player through sheer application and, most importantly, that he respected his limitations. More than anyone I have ever met, Geoff deliberated on how he should play. It became a conscious discipline and inevitably you wondered if he restricted himself too much; there were times when he showed glimpses of the man who could play raking shots and really attack the ball. For example, when Geoff toured Australia in 1979–80 he made a limited-overs century in a match in Sydney and went from 96 to three figures with an extra-cover drive off Dennis Lillee which contained more pure venom than any other shot I ever saw him play.

His reasons for opting out of the England Test side for a number of seasons have been guessed at and endlessly chewed over. I have no idea what his thinking was, but he had made real enemies and suffered via the suggestion that he was trying to avoid the fast bowlers around at the time. That shot against Lillee struck me as his way of getting back at the critics, the stroke of a man saying 'Up yours!' to the rest of the world. For Geoff Boycott, I reckon, it must have been a very satisfying moment.

MAX Walker, Australia's excellent medium-pacer of the '70s, was perhaps the most unnaturally-gifted bowler of all time. His run-up and delivery had all the appeal of a runaway tarantula; Max himself once described it as 'right arm over left earhole.' He bowled chest on, crossed his legs in delivery and bowled off the wrong foot. Just about everything was wrong in text-book terms. No-one could have imagined a bowler of his style — if that is what it was — had any sort of future in the game. But he became a wonderful Test bowler. Basically, I think, this was because he was an intelligent cricketer who looked around him and realised that in what was clearly an era of genuinely fast bowlers there was an opening for somebody who could swing the ball. Once he set out his stall to do that, and do it well, his extraordinary style worked in his favour.

A Test match at the Sydney Cricket Ground in January, 1973, will probably be remembered as Max's finest hour. Pakistan needed only 159 to win, which seemed a formality, so much so that I went into town on business instead of going to the game. Mid-afternoon I bumped into Ian Chappell, the Australian captain, who obviously had half a day off.

'Got them pretty quickly, did they?' I asked.

'No,' the skipper replied. 'We bloody well won. Maxie Walker bowled us to victory!'

It was an amazing feat: Max and Dennis Lillee bowled unchanged that day, with Max taking a remarkable 6–15, including a spell of five wickets for three runs off 30 deliveries. It was all over in 138 minutes. Lillee, incidentally, bowled despite a painful back, a typical example of what a fine competitor he was.

Max didn't always get a swag of wickets or a lot of publicity, but he was a very dangerous proposition once he got a hint. When the ball was swinging, he could be unplayable, and the lads hated facing him in the nets once he had the old inswinger going; they would stand there black and blue, having been hit repeatedly on the thigh, while Max grinned, nodded and did his best to hit them again. He was a thinking bowler who made use of every advantage he had. He used his head, planned his strategy and produced a very effective weapon out of one of the clumsiest bowling styles Test cricket has ever seen. Max Walker was a model in his own way.

Max's equivalent in the Australian team of the 1960s was Neil Hawke, another player who performed miracles with a bowling action which, quite frankly, would not have qualified him for first-grade club cricket on pure artistic merit. If anything, his style was even less appealing than Maxie's. He had an ungainly-looking approach, a chest-on action, and his left arm waved high in the air. Yet, Neil could swing the ball both ways more consistently than any Test bowler I've seen. He was the only quick bowler you would back consistently to go round the wicket and get lbw decisions with inswingers to right-handed batsmen. Neil was a gifted athlete and sportsman, but very much a self-made cricketer; his action should not have allowed him to bowl outswing, yet he did it expertly.

The key, once again, was that he thought about his bowling a lot more than a purely natural player might be inclined to do. Neil is a very intelligent bloke, who remains a thinker and philosopher about the game today. He was one of the first I am aware of who experimented consciously with different ways of gripping the ball — a totally different grip for slower deliveries, for instance. Modern bowlers such as Simon O'Donnell and especially Steve Waugh used such deception a lot in one-day cricket, but 'Hawkeye' did it a decade before one-day cricket became the fashion. He had more variety even then than Steve Waugh has now and would have made a fantastic one-day bowler; he was well ahead of his time.

Bowlers like Max Walker and Neil Hawke, unorthodox yet highly effective, bring home the message that coaches have to be careful in their philosophies. Unique skill, even if it breaks every rule in the book and some which haven't yet been invented, should never be discarded just because it is different. Being different makes a bowler unpredictable and batsmen at any level don't like that. Take a pairing like England's famous duo Fred Trueman and Brian Statham, for example. Between them they captured 559 wickets in Test cricket. Both fine and classical bowlers, both always capable of getting quality batsmen out. Fred, though, was the more likely to do it because his methods were a little more unpredictable. Brian wore you down, came at you all the time, but, unless you made a gross error of judgment, it was really only the one doing something off the seam that was liable to get you out. Fred's line and length were more unpredictable, but that was part of his method rather than a sign of waywardness. You never quite knew what to expect. But both men had the sort of delivery action that gave very few clues as to what was coming. And that, for a batsman, can be an absolute nightmare.

As a coach, I would never pre-judge a bowler on his action. I've long gone past that because I've seen too many bowlers with less-than-perfect actions who were supremely effective and met quite a few textbook trundlers who did absolutely nothing with the ball. Facing a bowler is obviously one way of finding out what he's up to but if you watch a bowler closely, preferably in a match situation, you can learn a lot. A simple rule is to watch whether batsmen have trouble picking up the length. If batsmen are playing back when they should be forward and viceversa, the bowler has something. Quite simply, judgment of length is the essence of batting; if you cannot judge the length of a delivery you have a problem.

IN my opinion Merv Hughes was one of the most underrated bowlers in the history of the game. The fact is that big Merv was a lot more than a hefty body and a trademark moustache: for an important period in Australian cricket, from late 1988 to 1993, he was the heart of the side, in many ways the inspiration of the team. Put a cricket ball in Merv's hands and he was always going to give you 150 per cent — fit or ailing, uphill or into the wind, on helpful tracks or on the ones that break some fast bowlers' hearts. There were times when I was Merv's biggest critic, but I was also his biggest fan. He was a great bloke to have in the side because he had a knack of making those around him respond and give a little bit more than they might sometimes have given. Because Merv did.

Anybody who walked through a local park and saw Merv staggering in to bowl would be inclined to scoff. 'No way, mate,' you might tell him. 'Give it away.' Yet, for a time he was just about the most feared fast bowler in the world. Batsmen might not rate him the quickest, certainly not the most athletic. Some were inclined not to admit to rating him at all because he did not look the part of the well-oiled fast bowling machine. But they recognised the body language and knew that Merv would always, always, come at them with everything he had. 'I don't want you there and I'm going to do everything I can to get rid of you. You'd better believe it!' Merv said that to them all, without even opening his mouth. Sure, he could say his piece; the old mo would quiver away and the crowd probably loved the idea that Merv was getting stuck into the enemy. However, he was brainier than some fast bowlers are supposed to be; I think the reason he attracted affection, while some Australian fast bowlers never did, was because there was always a bit of a twinkle and a grin.

'How many left?' asks Merv of an umpire.

'Three,' comes the reply.

'Is that three gone or three to come?' Whatever the imagery, Merv was nobody's fool.

He did not have a lot of what my generation calls common sense, but he was rarely short of a comment or an escapade to liven up the dressing room. Just having him around was an experience; he was a great influence and a monumental pest. His problem as far as his weight was concerned was that he was a glutton. It was part of the image, of course, to suggest that he was a huge drinker and Merv was not averse to hamming it up in a bar, playing to the gallery who assumed that because he was where he was and a bit over the top he had to be well into the booze. Merv liked a drink, but he was just as likely to go on the wagon for long periods if his weight looked like becoming a problem. While he was involved with Australia it was food, not booze, that put the centimetres round Merv's waist. I told him about it I don't know how many times and, sure, he was always going to be strong . . .

'My brain keeps telling me that what you say is right.' he'd explain. 'I'm being silly. Stop eating so much and I'll last longer. But then my guts butt in and say: "Oh, bugger off!"'

During one Test match in Adelaide, Errol Alcott and I were into him mercilessly. Watching what he ate, trying to cut him down. He went missing at tea, which is unusual and for Merv, pretty noticeable. One of the players dobbed him in and we found him in a cubicle in the toilet, sitting on the seat and eating the biggest plate of sandwiches you've ever seen. It all added up, and unfortunately he put a lot of extra strain on his body which eventually caught up with him.

He was a bigger nuisance than the flies and he loved it. I tried to make a point of never sitting in front of Merv on a plane trip because there was absolutely no chance of a quiet journey without a clip round the ear or a sudden pounding on the seat from behind. He told the world's corniest jokes and loved that, too. 'Simmo, the good news or the bad news? My old man's going to have a brain transplant. But he's thrilled to bits because he's going to get my brain and he reckons it's never been used before!!!' And Merv would curl up and just enjoy being Merv: the big, pounding heart of the side.

He was a formidable performer, no doubt about that. He was not in the Australian team just for his bonhomie or some sort of binding influence, though they were real enough. He was there on merit. On the 1989 Ashes tour he did not take a swag of wickets — 19 in six Tests, which is not outstanding as far as statistics go — but he took so many of the hard wickets. Terry Alderman was outstanding and rightly received most of the kudos, but if AB was ever in a bit of a corner he knew he could always throw the ball to Merv. And more often than not, Merv would take an important wicket and renew Australia's impetus. We did not hit a lot of trouble on that tour, but when we did it was reassuring to have Merv coming to the rescue. What captain could ask for more? He was also a great fieldsman, a fact often overlooked because he invariably patrolled the outfield where great dramas don't appear to happen. But if the ball went in the air, I'd as soon have Merv underneath it as anyone. In practice I would stretch him hard, perhaps 10 high catches in a row. He was always under the tenth, sweating his guts out and ready to go for the eleventh.

He was a big, brave and very resolute man. Not exactly a coach's dream but a personality any sensible coach and team valued very highly. He had great desire to play for Australia; that's what made him powerful.

I'll never forget his fabulously assertive performance against the West Indies in Perth in 1988–89, when Merv went into battle for the entire Australian nation after his team-mate, Geoff Lawson, was felled and badly injured by a Curtly Ambrose bouncer. He took 8–87, including a hat-trick, in the Windies second innings but he was more concerned with Lawson and the fact that Australia lost the match. Then there was Adelaide in 1990–91, against Pakistan, when Merv bowled on a knee which would have put most fast bowlers out of the match yet took 5–111 off 32 agonised overs in the second innings. Throughout, he needed injections before he could even walk, yet it never crossed his mind to tell anyone in the media. His team-mates whistled through their teeth and reflected yet again what a giant he was.

On top of all that, Merv could bat when the demand arose. Not with any great grace and finesse but with the same earthy conviction and courage that defined his bowling and made him an exceptional competitor. He used a 3lb 5oz bat which nobody else could lift, but he didn't have a backswing, and he deserves to be remembered for at least two outstanding innings: at Adelaide in 1989, when he scored an unbeaten 72 against the Windies, and on the Ashes tour later that year when he made 71 in the first, and perhaps decisive, Test at Headingley.

Inevitably, there are stories from these innings; stories that seem almost designed to mask the fact that Merv did a wonderful job. It would not surprise me to know he invented them to preserve his larrikin image but they and a hundred like them should be preserved. Dean Jones tells how Merv supported him during that match in Adelaide. Deano was 170 not out, and Merv came down the track and said: 'Don't worry, mate, I'll stick it out and you'll get your 200. Go for it.' Then Merv was hit inside the thigh, on the fingers, in the guts and finally on the back of the head. Dean raced down the pitch to make sure he was okay, and Merv cocked an eyebrow: 'Are you 200 yet?'

When Merv went out to bat at Headingley he joined Steve Waugh at a time when Steve was at the absolute peak of his form. Our reminders were simple: 'Don't do anything silly, just give Stephen a hand.' Merv took it all on board and promptly lifted Gooch over the top for six! 'What was going on?' AB asked later. 'Sorry skipper,' Merv replied, 'I was playing carefully, like you said and I just followed through a bit too strong.'

Merv Hughes will probably be remembered for his image rather than his 200-plus Test wickets — the big bloke with the bigger moustache doing warm-ups in front of his crowd at the MCG. A man who created affection from the public and warmed to them as readily as they warmed to him. An 'unstylist' who did the job with a ready wit and a larrikin approach to the game. I do not think he will object to that. However, it would be an injustice if, within that image, he is underrated as an international cricketer or as a figure of huge importance to Australia. I would say to any kid: if you think of Merv Hughes as a great character, you're right. Ask him for his autograph, he won't refuse. And, despite the bullshit he will probably give you, don't ever forget he was also a fine international bowler, in his own way and in his own time one of the very, very best.

CHAPTER 7

Limited-overs cricket is the future of the game. I can hear the howls of protest from traditionalists and I understand their concern for first-class and Test matches which, like them, I consider to be the most important forms of cricket. However, they so often base their fears on the assumption that limited-overs and 'traditional' cricket are fundamentally in competition — and I simply do not agree with that view.

Take cricket as a game in all its forms and blind Freddie can see that limited-overs is the most important promotional vehicle we have. In very simple terms, I believe that limited-overs cricket provides an introduction to the game for thousands and potentially millions of people who might otherwise never watch a match. It provides colour and excitement, instant solutions in an instant world and a wonderful opportunity for cricket's administrators to popularise one form of the game and reap the interest in another.

First-class cricket and Test matches still represent the ultimate in the game, for the players and for those spectators who have learned cricket's subtle skills and enjoy the mind games involved. There is nothing wrong with that and no reason, I believe, why that should not continue. However, the opportunity to expand the game beyond the old Commonwealth countries and into parts of the world where it is still a foreign language is provided by the limited-overs format. This has to be exploited, not just to ensure cricket's survival, but to make it a genuine alternative to future generations who have a lot more sports, games and pastimes to chose from than we ever did. As for the basic simplicity of the one-day game — the accusation that it really isn't proper cricket at all — I bet more people played draughts before chess than the other way round.

Fiddle with one-day cricket by all means. Change the match regulations and the format to respond to what the public appears to want. The use of fielding circles was a masterstroke in terms of crowd entertainment and there is no reason why the rules should not be adjusted further from time to time. More fieldsmen closer to the bat for longer; interchange of players allowing for specialist fieldsmen or different types of bowlers to be used; bring in more switch-hitters; pull in the boundaries so that there are more fours and sixes. Take any of these options if that is what the game seems to need.

I am not advocating all this in the near future; I'm not even saying it must happen. The limited-overs game is pretty popular in its present format and there's no earthly reason to change it just for the sake of novelty. What I do believe, however, is that the Australian Cricket Board and international administrators should have a whole set of possibilities and alternatives just waiting to be put into place if there are signs that the game is starting to lose its popularity. The bottom line is that one-day cricket has become the game's promotional arm. Every idea is worth considering and none should be rejected simply on the grounds that it breaks with traditionally-held views.

Limited-overs cricket is not new. It has been hugely popularised by television, but it did not begin with the box. In fact, there is plenty of evidence of (lucrative) one-day matches being played a century ago! It is worth having a look at the development of modern limited-overs cricket, because it shows how one-day and the first-class game have profited from each other. That, at least, was the experience of those of us involved in matches organised by an English journalist, the late Ron Roberts, and sponsored by the tobacco company, Rothmans, in the early 1960s.

The idea of taking a 'circus' of established and emerging players on tour to various countries was pretty revolutionary at that time, and fairly low-key except for the people involved. But it was very well received everywhere we went. I trekked off to Zimbabwe (or to be more precise, Rhodesia, as it was known in those days), South Africa, Hong Kong, New Zealand, India and Kenya, and had a wonderful chance to broaden my experience among some of the world's finest players.

My first captain on these tours was one of England's finest ever batsmen, Denis Compton, the 'Brylcream Boy' of his time, a pop star before pop stars were invented. Punctuality was never Denis' strong suit and he was once said to have been surprised to learn from his car radio that a Test match at the Oval — in which he was taking part — had started early and was under way. I'll never forget his first words to me: 'What you have to remember young Simpson is that your job over here is to score runs and my job is to teach you how to enjoy cricket.' He certainly did that.

The tours were great ambassadors for cricket in that they brought the game and its personalities within reach. The game benefited because players of different nations had the chance to share the same dressing room and talk honestly about the issues of the day. We were all inclined to be protective of our own players, naturally enough, when we were in competition. But sitting as team-mates we talked frankly — about chucking, one of the major cricket issues of the time, for instance — and developed a spirit of really wanting to do something for the good of the game as a whole. It was probably the first time there had been a real interchange of ideas between players of different countries on tour together.

Back in England, Roberts and Compton's manager, Bagenal Harvey, decided they were on to a winner. They devised a 'limited-overs format' of 40 six-ball overs a side, rustled up a mixture of well-known and emerging players known as the 'Rothmans Cavaliers', and staged regular matches around the country. Instant success. I remember we played a match in Birmingham for the Warwickshire beneficiary Jack Bannister — who once took 10 wickets in an innings and later became a media commentator — and attracted over 13,000 people. This was a huge crowd for a new concept in those days. The BBC quickly came to the party by agreeing to televise the second innings of the games — quite a coup in itself — and the reaction was so positive that the English counties quickly claimed a piece of the action for themselves. The limited-overs Gillette Cup was introduced in 1963 and inside 10 years there were two other popular one-day competitions played every English season.

The game has changed enormously since the Cavaliers reinvented it for modern times. At first the one-day matches were a relaxation, a bit of relief from the everyday disciplines of playing cricket for a living. Apart from any other consideration, I suppose, the players were paid for taking part, rather than on results. Playing 'entertaining' cricket shouldn't be too difficult under those circumstances. Batsmen were expected to swing from the ding and score lots of runs, bowlers were expected to provide a bit of cannon fodder, while fieldsmen hurled themselves about a bit more than they normally would but generally did not risk life and limb. It was good-natured stuff played within the bounds of professional self-respect, but never to the point of pistols at dawn. Initially, this attitude extended a little bit into the international arena, which is why, I believe, it took so long to be accepted in Australia. For many years, our record was nothing to write home about — even when I became involved with the Australian team as assistant manager and then coach, there were some players who were still to be convinced that they needed to treat limited-overs cricket seriously. Mind you, by then the public were already smitten by it.

One of the first exercises I did when I became coach was to analyse the one-day game from every point of view. It didn't take long for me to realise that it was the simplest form of the game I had ever seen. The team which scored at a-run-a-ball was going to win 99.9 per cent of every limited-overs match ever played. Cut through all the baloney and bulldust, that was a fact.

Attacking the game as a simple, manageable equation was the way Australia became the best one-day side in the world. It took individual talent, a hell of a lot of hard work, and personal courage and commitment in all kinds of pressure situations. The Australian players responded magnificently. So far as it was possible to prepare, train and approach one-day cricket with a winning philosophy, Australia had the right formula and applied it brilliantly. Nobody wins 'em all, but Australia's expertise between the World Cup we won in 1987 and the one we lost foolishly four years later was a model for the rest of the world. We set a standard which will be hard to beat.

It is fashionable to talk about one-day and first-class cricket as though they are entirely different games, requiring quite different skills and approaches. That is nonsense. I have always been convinced that the best players will tackle either form of the game successfully, simply because they have the skills and mental attitude which make them the best. Attitude and aptitude are what count. We hear a lot about so-and-so being a 'one-day player' and, of course, there are players whose natural style is well suited to the limited-overs game. But they have to be good at their job, they have to be accomplished cricketers first.

When we looked closely at what limited-overs cricket was all about we quickly realised that a lot of it came down to attitude, to being mentally aggressive at the crease or in the field. So we made that a strong part of our game-plan: be mentally aggressive, never miss the opportunity to score. A-run-a-ball, the basic philosophy, was broken down into milestones. In normal circumstances, after 25 overs, we wanted to have scored around 100 runs, and be ready to accelerate. Six an over from that point was acceptable, but we would be looking for bonuses on top of that; and definitely at least 60 off the last 10 overs (though, more often than not, we scored 80 or 90). Not losing wickets was also a fundamental part of the formula; it was essential to have wickets in hand for the last 15 overs or so, so we could capitalise on what we'd scored and orchestrate a dash for home. Be energetic mentally and physically, run well between the wickets, take on the fieldsmen whenever possible, look for accurate placement through the gaps, keep men in reserve for the death...

All pretty simple, really, and one of the delights of our style was that it rarely relied on slogging for effect. In fact, I don't believe one-day cricket is about slogging; it is about cool, efficient batting. It is no coincidence that the high-quality Test batsmen have usually been very good one-day players. Probably the best I have seen was New Zealand's Glenn Turner — hardly the epitome of a rob-and-pillage merchant, but a bloke with a marvellous facility for caressing the ball through the gaps. Glenn never tried to hit the skin off the ball, he just steered and chipped and glided it around and he was wonderfully effective.

Bring that attitude up to date and you have a player like Ian Healy. Often underestimated — perhaps because he does not flog every ball out of the ground — but a wonderful one-day player in his own right. I do not claim that statistics prove everything but they say a lot about the one-day game and Healy's strike rate is extremely high. He is a hustler, a worker and chipper of the ball, and there are not many deliveries off which he does not score. The really big grounds suit Healy's style, because he does not hit the ball hard or far enough to be caught in the distant outfield; instead he falls short of the fieldsmen and picks up a mass of twos and threes.

Incidentally, the more I looked at the requirements of one-day cricket, the more it struck me that it would have been an ideal game for a couple of opening batsmen called Simpson and Lawry — pretty slick between the wickets, good movers and workers of the ball. Bill and I only played one limited-overs match together, for Australia against Sussex (as winners of the English Gillette Cup) while we were on tour in 1964. We played our normal game and then Peter Burge played his normal game and we won quite comfortably.

As captain of Australia during the World Series split, I played in two one-day internationals against the West Indies, at St Johns and Castries in 1978, and won a man-of-the-match award. At 42 years and 68 days, R. B. Simpson is the oldest player to represent Australia in limited-overs internationals. And likely to remain so.

Our bowling strategy was based on the belief that it was important to bowl sides out. We never went into a match with the aim of containment. Early wickets put pressure on the opposition batsmen and a steady trickle of wickets wrecks the best-laid plans of any opponent. So our bowlers looked for wickets and our fieldsmen were aggressive and positive; nobody expected a reprimand for trying to take a wicket, even if a throw went astray or a catching attempt failed. We had the class to take wickets and screw down the pressure and nobody exemplified that better than Simon O'Donnell, Simon Davis and Steve Waugh. In some ways, they revolutionised the bowlers' approach to one-day games.

Simon O'Donnell has a deserved reputation for having been a model one-day player and a lot of it was based on those memorable occasions when he went out and belted quick runs, usually over the fence, with the crowd going wild. However, he was more valuable to the team as a bowler. As far as we were concerned, he was a bowler who batted and it is interesting that he finished his 87-match career with 1242 runs and 108 wickets.

Steve Waugh became the 'Iceman' after his performances in the 1987 World Cup, when he was bowled some superb overs at the end of our opponents' innings, and that is a bigger compliment than many people appreciate. Bowling at the death is not easy, and there are many very good bowlers, with all the skills and plenty of character, who can't do it well. Never underestimate the courage it takes to bowl to a plan, to refuse to be diverted whatever the batsman's reaction, to keep your nerve when there is every indication that a packed stadium has gone totally berserk. Steve became our specialist during the '87 World Cup and won matches under extraordinary pressure with his ability to camouflage a change of pace and bowl a magnificent yorker length apparently at will. Steve's normal pace is quicker than his action suggests and surprises a lot of batsmen; that and his subtle changes of pace are the key to his outstanding effectiveness in one-day cricket.

Whatever the make-up of the side, we always set out to bowl sides out as cheaply as possible. It was not all that long ago that spinners were regarded as a luxury in limited-overs cricket, especially in England where the grounds are generally small and there was a fear, perhaps justified, that unremarkable spinners would be slogged expensively.

Australia was fortunate in that respect because for a number of years in the late '80s and early '90s we had Peter Taylor, unquestionably the best one-day off-spinner I have seen, who we could play in the side without compromising our belief in taking wickets. Peter's attitude was as aggressive as any fast bowler. Not only did he keep it tight but he took wickets — bowled, return catches, caught behind the wicket — genuine bowler's wickets that were not the product of a mistimed slog at a poor delivery. He had excellent variety without losing control and it was very rare for him to concede more than 40 runs, or fail to take a wicket, even though he was often bowling under pressure. Peter Taylor was a quality bowler backed, like his colleagues, by fielding which was as good as the world of cricket has ever seen.

Matches stand out, of course. In 1990, we played a triangular tournament in New Zealand and won 5–0, defeating New Zealand three times and India twice; I reckon our performances match by match were really special. I don't believe any side has played better one-day cricket than we produced consistently during that series. The fielding was exceptional, the batting was controlled and we bowled out the opposition three times, to prove just how positive our attitude was. Almost exactly a year after that we won the one-day series on our Caribbean tour, and if I had to pick a match which summed up just how complete a side Australia had become I'd nominate the one at Queen's Park Oval, Port of Spain, Trinidad.

The start was delayed by rain, there was a good deal of cynical fiddling with the overs after Australia were put in and, although the match was supposed to be 42 overs a side, the Windies bowled only 34. Australia made 9–172, not a huge target on the face of it against a Windies team stacked with batsmen, but from the moment they went in our bowling and outfielding were absolutely magnificent. Only three of their batsmen, Desmond Haynes, Phil Simmons and Viv Richards, reached double figures and although Simmons and Richards each hit a six there was never the slightest hint of a panic in the field. The players were furious at what they saw as deliberate manipulation of the over-rate by the Windies, yet they kept cool and played with total professionalism. Watching the Windies' innings being strangled — they were eventually beaten by 45 runs with 17 deliveries to spare — a lot of seasoned observers wondered if any team had ever played the limited-overs game as expertly as Australia had done that day. Watching the boys in action was quite an experience.

Between February 23, 1990 and March 9, a year later, Australia won 21 and lost two of 23 matches. One of those losses, against New Zealand in Hobart, was by one run. Quite a record!

Creating a standard like that takes a lot of hard work. There is no magic formula. Other countries know what the requirements of one-day cricket are, but they do not consistently match Australia's expertise and one reason for that may be the fact that the limited-overs format and atmosphere suits our character. We are hustlers, always at our best when we are striving and pushing ourselves. In a technical sense the English and West Indian players often time the ball better than we do. But, while English players are marvellous at hitting the loose ball fluently, they are pretty hopeless at batting under pressure.

The real difference between Test cricket and international one-day matches is the intensity of the shorter game. You go harder, quicker. Whatever the quality of the opposition, you have to bat against the run-rate and that imposes pressure in itself. Play out a maiden over, or hit two solid shots straight to fieldsmen, or fail to score for a couple of overs, and suddenly the sweat is trickling down a batsman's neck. Good bowling and fielding produces such pressure, but so does the intensity of the game. It is a simple game, but not an easy one.

Whenever the Australian team met before a one-day match there was always a great emphasis on words such as concentration and enjoyment but especially on energy, energy, energy. Tough running between the wickets, strike rotation, all the basics we know are the key to the game. But especially energy, mental and physical.

This was precisely what was missing from our World Cup campaign in 1992. Of course, this is easy to say now, but it was hard to live with and understand then. We were absolutely flat, that much was clear, but the reasons why are not as easy to define. Our previous one-day tournament was the triangular World Series against India and West Indies, which we won 7–2, so our form was obviously good and our confidence high. However, between that competition and the Cup we played the final two Tests of our home series against India, so we went into the Cup with only a few days break and no chance to readjust.

Perhaps we were living on our one-day form, perhaps we were a bit over-confident. It's possible — for four years we had lifted ourselves in one-day matches whatever the circumstances or the difficulties and maybe we simply waited for it to happen again. Switching from Test cricket to the one-day game had never been a big problem for us, in fact we were proud of our ability to make the transition. We had so much experience, so much background. But, suddenly, New Zealand hit us with new tactics and we just did not respond; by the time we began to get some real intensity into our game we were struggling to qualify — having said that, however, we were only one match from making the semi-finals and it could be argued that the eventual winners, Pakistan, got there by default.

I say this because their match against England in Adelaide was rained off, with Pakistan poised to lose. The point they received from the wash-out was enough to put them into the semi-finals ahead of Australia. In fact, Pakistan played very ordinary cricket until the last two matches of that World Cup, the two that mattered. Them's the breaks, especially in the one-day game. Still, it's worth remembering that Pakistan did not reach the final through some master plan or superior strategy. In the semis, and then the final against England, they played some outstanding cricket.

New Zealand took everybody, not just Australia, by surprise, by opening their bowling attack with the off-spinner, Dipak Patel, and instructing their opening batsmen to belt anything within reach in the early overs. It worked for them in home conditions and full marks for the way they went about it; with nothing to lose, New Zealand went for broke. However, it should be remembered that they didn't actually reach the final, so it is hard to argue that their way was the best way, much less the only way, to tackle a one-day match.

I have found that if a new tactic is seen to work in one-day cricket there is inevitably a tendency to jump on that strategy's bandwagon. In this case, I believe that the Kiwis' approach was a bit desperate. It was brilliantly conceived and it worked for them, up to a point, in their own conditions. However, I don't think it would have worked on Australia's quicker pitches. Our openers, Geoff Marsh and David Boon, weren't at their best against slow bowling early on and we found the novelty of New Zealand's approach hard to combat. They got the jump on us, no doubt about it, but it was soon being suggested that we had our tactics all wrong. We were too conservative, not flexible or imaginative enough, blah, blah, blah. But I would back our players' approach any time and, four years later, we reached the World Cup final again.

Our problem in 1992 was not that our philosophy was wrong, but simply that our application was very, very poor. We did not play nearly as well as we could, but a drop in form can occur at any time. You just hope that it doesn't affect too many players at the same moment and that the timing is not too expensive. The 1992 World Cup was simply not the time.

There are a couple of myths about one-day cricket which deserve to be exploded and I think Australia's general approach to the game has helped to do that over the years. There will always be room for manoeuvre and flexibility, for taking a chance and trying to exploit a situation with a different approach. But I hear a lot of labels attached to the limited-overs game which do not really bear analysis. One is that it is a game for big-hitters, for sloggers if you like. Rubbish! It will always be a game for good cricketers who are good at shot-selection and who know how to pace an innings. That is why I do not think that limited-overs cricket seriously threatens the integrity of the 'proper' game. Then there is the myth that one-day cricket is always exciting. Let's be honest, boring cricket is boring cricket whether it is played over a number of days or a number of overs.

The rules of one-day cricket are designed to produce a close finish. That is what gives the format most of its spectator appeal and because professionals are pretty shrewd and competitive, interest is usually maintained until the last few overs of the game. But not always. Let's not pretend that every limited-overs match is fought on a knife edge. When I regularly did radio and television commentary on one-day matches I swear I could have gone to sleep for 10 or 15 overs, and then woken up and picked up the thread of the game without missing anything. If a game unfolds like that it is a real bore. The side batting first makes a poor score and the result becomes a foregone conclusion. Or the side chasing a score collapses, the target becomes unachievable and nobody has anywhere to go. It's not as though you can play for a draw and have the satisfaction of denying the other side a victory. Television tries to keep the interest going by insisting that anything can happen in the one-day game — and goodness knows, that has been proved often enough — but matches which meander through a predictable formula to a predictable result are an instant pain.

Ironically, the Australian team have sometimes been criticised for being dull because they are too efficient at the one-day game. I'll accept the compliment, but I don't follow the reasoning. The best golfers hit a drive down the middle, drop their second shot next to the pin and sink the birdie putt, time after time after time… they hope. The closer to perfection the better and very exciting to watch. Call it clinical if you like, but what's wrong with excitement generated by excellence. One-day cricket really does not need a shower of fours and sixes for its entertainment value; I remember a match against West Indies in Sydney when Australia made 9–101 and then won by 14 runs! Not a lot of boundaries there, but not a soul left the ground before the final delivery. A great imbalance between bat and ball is far duller than a hard-fought match with low scores; the attraction of one side thumping a huge, impossible target soon wanes.

There is also a myth, probably created by the English style of playing one-day cricket, that the best, even the only approach to bowling is line and length. The very idea is defensive, which is a bad mindset for a start. Military line-and-length bowling is probably the easiest to hit, especially in the last 15 overs or so when batsmen are looking to build a score or win the match. Anything predictable then is usually fatal. Accuracy is important, of course, but there has to be flexibility as well, otherwise the bowler is going to be slogged. Variation and change of pace are vital. . . that's why Steve Waugh has been so effective as a bowler in the last overs of limited-overs matches, because he above all bowlers has the ability to mix up his deliveries and bowl the unexpected without sacrificing accuracy. The important thing is to keep applying pressure and there is always more pressure on the batsman who doesn't quite know what's coming next. Not that I am dismissing consistent accuracy as a vital factor; the ability to bowl yorker-length is priceless and Australia's Glenn McGrath's skill in this area is one reason he is developing into one of the outstanding bowlers in the limited-overs game.

An important factor in the 'death' overs is that the white ball scuffs more — without any help from the players, I might add — and tends to swing 'Irish' more as it gets older. Several good bowlers have learned to use this to their advantage and thinking teams work on keeping one side of the ball as smooth as possible ready for the last overs. Bowlers like McGrath, Waqar Younis and Wasim Akram have the ability to swing the ball quick and late, and are far more difficult to score off than medium-pacers who are just trying to bowl dot balls.

Spinners have a role, too, particularly because the good ones have the capacity to vary flight, length and the amount of spin they put on the ball. There is an image of the spinner in one-day cricket as a fill-in bowler delivering darts as fast as possible, but no really accomplished spinner needs to bowl like that. Once again, this thinking probably developed in England where the grounds are small and spinners were afraid of being slogged — especially some very ordinary spinners who lacked control and variation. In fact, spin bowling in the one-day game calls for even more flight and more subtleties, because there is no 'wearing-down' factor. Shane Warne is a very effective one-day bowler without sacrificing his tricks, as is India's Anil Kumble, while other genuine spinners such as Peter Taylor and England's John Emburey have had plenty of scope to show their skills.

Let me reiterate that the popularity of one-day cricket does not offend the purist in me at all — because I regard it as the promotional arm of the game as a whole and a potential bridge between people who might otherwise never watch cricket. The one-day stuff has already popularised cricket in far-off places and I really believe that more should be done to take it into countries which have no traditional attachment to the game. No point in taking a Test match to China for public consumption; the crowd would not have the faintest idea what they were supposed to be watching. But one-day matches, simplified even further if necessary, could do an enormous amount to spread the gospel and kindle an interest. Why not play a form of the game without any lbw to begin with? The important thing is to get spectators into the ground; how you get them there is of less importance. Introduce the game, get it accepted and then enlarge it. The trail has already been blazed — well, fanned a bit — by a team I took to China some years ago.

It was a fascinating experience for the players, mostly ex-internationals who split into two mixed teams, and the crowds obviously enjoyed the matches we played even if the intricacies were lost on them. They were familiar with baseball, so a lot of the cricket action made sense: bowled was being struck out, catches and run-outs looked familiar. The lbw concept, though, clearly made no sense at all.

We turned up at one village where a match had been advertised, and despite the fact it was bucketing down with rain there were 6000 spectators already in the stands! So we turned out in the rain, gave a 'Kanga Cricket' sort of exhibition, and invited the kids to have a go. (Kanga cricket was a special junior development program introduced in Australia a few years back, which involves 'mock' cricket games using plastic stumps and bats, a softer ball, improvised pitches — as in just about any open space — and is designed to introduce youngsters to the fundamentals, and the simple pleasures, of the game.) In no time at all there were hundreds of them on the field. One little bloke, who looked about eight years old, obviously had very natural ball skills and as soon as we showed him the basics of batting and bowling he took to it like a (Peking?) duck to water. When this young fella hit a particularly nice shot for four, Dougie Walters went up and shook his hand — so every time he hit a boundary after that the kid went round shaking hands. He thought it was part of the conventions of the game!

As geographically huge as China is, there seems to be very little public open space. It's as if every centimetre is taken up with growing something. At least, that's the impression we got, admittedly from a very limited view of the country. But then, Kanga Cricket doesn't take up a lot of space; so why not give it a go?

IT IS SOMETHING OF A CLICHE THESE DAYS TO TALK ABOUT THE COMPETITION CRICKET FACES FROM OTHER SPORTS, THE ALTERNATIVE PASTIMES OPEN TO THE YOUNG GENERATION. The conclusion is usually that cricket is fighting for its life. That is true in a sense and there's no room for complacency if the game is to prosper but I have been hearing gloomy stories about cricket being in decline ever since I can remember and it still looks pretty healthy to me. One way in which coaches can be affected by the mood of anxiety in some quarters is to embark on the search for the 'attractive' batsman. Every batsman has to 'entertain', every batsman has to be a strokemaker. Trying to coach these qualities is as false as attempting to make every batsman a master of forward defence; it is rank bad coaching to even attempt to make everybody the same. Coaches should not be in the business of marketing clones.

If I had my way I would not involve youngsters in competitive cricket until the age of about 13. I'd teach them the basics of grip and stance and then let them go out and have a good time, just hitting the ball, fielding and bowling enthusiastically. Above all, they should be enjoying the game. Naturally, they would play in teams and there is nothing wrong with rewarding good play or consistent effort over a season, but there is a danger — which over-demanding parents sometimes accentuate — of making kids play the game just for the sake of winning trophies. These days, so many kids find themselves playing competition sport from a very early age and it's no wonder that they drop out at the 'rebellious' age of their mid-teens.

There are a lot of alternatives open to youngsters these days and they will eventually stick with what they enjoy, so encouraging a love of cricket is more important than teaching technicalities at an early age. Teach them the barest of fundamentals and then put them in an atmosphere where they can really learn to love the game. Children are naturally competitive and I think that, deep down, we all want to encourage that, but it is a mistake to teach cricket in a confined structure where the sheer enjoyment of the game is lost.

The game has been spread internationally in recent seasons, but in my opinion not nearly wide enough. It is great to see the development of teams like Sri Lanka and Zimbabwe, while a lot of quality cricket is now played in Holland, Denmark, Canada, Bermuda and the USA. And who can forget Kenya's impact on the 1996 World Cup, when they defeated the mighty West Indies in one of cricket's most stunning upsets? However, I feel organised cricket is not really doing enough to spread the word and challenge the myth that cricket is a stuffy pastime played between pauses for tea and cucumber sandwiches. We have to get off our butts and promote the sport as a genuinely international game — and limited-overs cricket is the way to do it. Don't like razzamatazz? I find basketball to be the dullest game imaginable — nothing happening in the middle of the court, miss or score a basket, chase to the other end — but it is well sold and the hype makes it an exciting spectacle. Baseball can be a slow game, but it is presented as a family day out, and there always seems to be plenty happening on the sidelines. Cricket can learn from these sports — not follow them slavishly, but it would do well to pick up the genuine selling points.

I am delighted that the 1998 Commonwealth Games, in Malaysia, will, for the first time, include cricket. Say what you like about the Games ethic, this added exposure for cricket can only be for the better. Seven- or eight-a-side cricket is now being tried in Hong Kong — I think that six-a-side is better — and on small grounds it has enormous appeal. It would be no good trying to play such a game on a vast area like the MCG, because the fieldsmen would run themselves into the ground in no time, but a tight arena like the one at Kowloon in Hong Kong is ideal. Such a limited form of limited-overs cricket could well be the way to introduce the game into Asia. It is certainly worth a try.

A couple of asides from that China trip, both involving Dougie Walters, who has his own, very individualistic view of what's going on around him. We naturally had to make a visit to the Great Wall — one of the Wonders of the World and the only man-made artefact visible from outer space. Such a venture is what the modern advertising men would call a 'must-see' experience. Dougie made the two-hour bus journey with the rest of us but when we arrived, he didn't move. Instead, he sat on the bus, tinny in one hand, cigarette in the other, perfectly content.

'Seen one wall, you've seen 'em all,' he explained.

Later on, in Hong Kong, it was blowing a gale as we returned by junk from a harbour trip. Most of us were huddled inside, clinging on for dear life, but Dougie decided to go for a walk on deck. Sure enough, the next time the boat lurched madly, he disappeared over the side. Dougie cannot swim, which probably would not have mattered that much in such a storm-tossed sea, but it didn't help. Fortunately, though, one of the crew saw him fall and had the presence of mind to grab a boat-hook before Dougie disappeared into the night. Up comes Dougie, I swear with a beer still in his hand.

'Bloody salty down there, y'know… '

Cricket has so many different ways of promoting itself. I remember back in 1968 when the entrepreneur Jack Neary — still a dynamic figure in the entertainment world — and I helped set up a double-wicket competition which was played at different venues across Australia and involved top players from all around the world. Single-wicket tournaments were not new, but double-wicket had more of a 'team' feel about it, at least that's the way Jack and I approached the concept. For the first time, we paid international cricketers very good money to tour Australia. The matches were televised by Sydney's Channel Seven and consequently created enormous interest, not least because there were some mighty impressive players on show: Wes Hall and Charlie Griffith, Rohan Kanhai and Garfield Sobers from the West Indies; from England we had Basil D'Oliveira, Fred Trueman, Ken Barrington and Colin Milburn; the Pollock brothers, Trevor Goddard and Denis Lindsay arrived from South Africa; and Bill Lawry, Doug Walters, Graham McKenzie and myself were the Australians. The matches were played over a maximum of eight overs per side — if a wicket fell, the other batsman continued on, facing every ball. The eventual winners were Hall and Sobers, though I like to think the biggest victor was the game itself, which must have benefited from the publicity the series generated.

For many years, the brewing company, Tooheys, sponsored a country cricket circuit in NSW which took advantage of the popularity of the one-day game to further cricket's appeal and at the same time repay the hardworking country areas for all the effort they put into the game's development. Half a dozen first-class players, split among two country sides, played in matches played on synthetic surfaces (where necessary) and enjoyed a great atmosphere. And since Tooheys picked up the bill, there was a genuine financial return to the local associations. The list of very fine players who came from the bush to play for Australia is unending — the game owes the country boys a great deal. I recall one recent season, for example, when there were 48 players in Sydney grade cricket who had been recruited from the country. A bloke like Michael Slater, who grew up in Wagga Wagga, received some of his grounding in the game from attending Tooheys coaching clinics.

Tooheys provided the cash, the local associations and players provided the organisation, and the matches took on a real carnival atmosphere. Special events were organised around the cricket. Local radio stations broadcast ball-by-ball commentary, there were 'breakfast with the stars' functions, all kinds of promotional stuff. In one match, Canberra played Goulburn in front of 16,000 spectators at Bruce Stadium in Canberra. The sense of occasion was tremendous and the local associations enjoyed a big boost to their finances. Cricket really was on show. If matches like that can be organised in country Australia, why not in China? Is the idea really that far-fetched?

Exposure is the key: giving kids the opportunity to involve themselves in the game. I'm confident that from this will grow a real interest in first-class cricket and in Test matches. I have heard all the stories about limited-overs cricket destroying the real thing and while this has to be a possibility, it is not a strong one. One-day cricket is often used as an excuse by professional cricketers themselves to explain away poor technique, but that is a cop-out I simply don't accept. The excuse is most often trotted out by English players who don't have the skills or mental application to play one-day cricket properly, but still need a scapegoat for their poor performances at Test level. For mine, it is a thin attempt to vindicate mediocrity.

The young generation now see limited-overs cricket as a glamour sport. They associate with their heroes at the grounds, through the media and, importantly, through colour television which has had an enormous impact. The players of a couple of generations ago were little more than shadows on a black-and-white screen; now colour reflects the personality of the players and makes them a bit larger than life. Television exposure has opened up the game to more women and made it a real family event in an age when there is fierce competition for the family dollar. The promotional value of a bloke such as Shane Warne simply cannot be overestimated in a modern society built on the cult of personality. No cricketer with the exception of Bradman has developed a celebrity status in the eyes of youngsters to rival the regard they have for Shane. It is quite a thought.

A few years ago, I was struck by the number of young people queuing outside the SCG for a one-day international. Jeans, long hair, crazy fashions... thousands of them, all having a great time. The next night I drove past a pop concert in the park and the same kids were there, wearing the same gear, all having a similarly great time. They were attending an 'event'; cricket one day, pop music the next. That is their culture and sport needs to be very much a part of it. Limited-overs cricket is an event and that seems to offend some critics.

However, it is an event which will steer youngsters towards the game and help preserve it at all levels for future generations of players and spectators. And we should never complain about that.

Some players create a huge amount of publicity right through their careers. Perhaps this is because they attract the media as characters, as saleable personalities. Perhaps it is because they are so naturally gifted that constant recognition is inevitable. Besides, these cricketers are players who are regarded as great blokes and great influences by their team-mates, even when the media spotlight is elsewhere. Let's call them the 'players' players' and look at just a handful…

IN my opinion, the Australian selectors who dropped David Boon from the Australian one-day side in 1995–96 lost faith in the champion Tasmanian at least a season too early. He would have been a wonderful asset in the '96 World Cup. I believe his record insisted that he still had a lot to offer, especially since his style was a perfect complement to the strokemakers in the Australian side. Hindsight is a wonderful thing but, on reflection, we probably took too many strokemakers to the sub-continent for the World Cup; a player of David's experience and ability would have given us an important extra dimension. One-day cricket is not all about purple strokes, it is also about the ability to build partnerships and big totals, and to pace your game. Strokemakers, by definition, tend to need a high percentage of the strike, so two at the crease together is not the best combination, exciting as it can be to watch.

Boonie was probably the best batsman in the world in the early 1990s, but he was rarely given the credit he deserved except by those close enough to the side to appreciate fully how valuable he was in the team set-up. The media can make a legend out of a one-off performance, but Boonie's contribution to Australian cricket spanned some of the toughest years of modern times. He did it the hard way right from his apprenticeship in Tasmania, at a time when cricket there was at a low ebb and he had very few experienced hands to help him along. Very ordinary cricketers were moving down from Sydney and Melbourne and getting a game in the Tasmania team, so Boonie really had to set his own standards.

David broke into Australian cricket at a difficult time — South African defections, the early captaincy of Allan Border, an unsuccessful Ashes tour in 1985 — and he was later dropped from the side after a poor series against England at home. But it was typical of the man that he took all the setbacks on the chin, became more determined than ever to succeed, and eventually became one of the most valuable batsmen in the world. It was no coincidence that Boon was the Player of the Final when Australia won the World Cup in Calcutta in 1987; in that instance, at least, he received the recognition he deserved.

Boonie was always a huge favourite in India and Pakistan, where conditions are tough and the cricket fanatics have a deep admiration for the bloke who sees the job through to the end. He was invariably the player first recognised and most sought after, and during the 1996 World Cup the question most asked of us was: 'Where's Bun? How could you possibly leave him behind?' As far as they were concerned, the team wasn't Australia without the 'Keg on Legs'.

His build reflected his character — square and solid with a strong face which rarely showed a lot of expression, whether he was battling for survival or acknowledging the applause for a century. He looked a bit portlier than he really was and it was a matter of great pride to him that when the players were tested for excess body fat before the season, his was invariably one of the best results. He liked a tinny or two, however, there's no disputing that, and there is a strong rumour that he made a successful attempt on the world tinny record on the flight to England in 1989. All kinds of figures are bandied about concerning that 'achievement', usually starting at around 50! All I can say is that, unlike a previous claimant to the record, Boon actually walked off the plane at Heathrow, although he did look a little under the weather. Airsick, I suppose.

One of the great memories of Boonie will always be his leadership of the victory celebrations in the dressing room — perched on a table, can in hand, booming out the Australian victory verse. The sound of Boonie bellowing the Australian team victory song still reverberates around Lord's and scandalises the MCC members.

He succeeded because he worked at it. I first got to know David Boon on the 1986 tour to New Zealand, where I was asked to have a look at the team with a view to taking on a coaching role. Some of the players' attitudes were well below what they should have been, but there was no problem with Boonie or his great mate, Geoff Marsh. They were mad keen to improve their game and I remember spending hours under a huge oak tree on the boundary at Hamilton hitting balls for them to catch. Hundreds, probably thousands. Marsh went from being an original 'iron hands' to become a magnificent gully fieldsman, while Boonie finished up as the best short leg in the game. Nobody deserved success more.

David had a dreadful Ashes series in 1986–87 when his technique became so flawed that he gave catching practice virtually whenever he played forward. He was dropped from the side, but worked at his problems and came back a much more complete and commanding player. In the great years to follow he still had to work hard to prevent himself falling back into bad habits, but he was never afraid of hard work. And he was so conscientious that he rarely left the nets without checking with me that his front foot was pointing in the right direction. Just to make sure.

He was a strong, durable man, uncomplaining and physically brave. The West Indies respected him as a fearless competitor, one of the batsmen in world cricket who would never take a backward step — and they had a list of names of those they knew they could intimidate. He earned his reputation with deeds, not with his mouth, but he could hold his own against any bowler who went over the top with the verbals. When he made a comment it was usually short and cutting, like the day in Barbados when feeling was running high and their opening batsman, Desmond Haynes, thought he had something in his eye. He approached Boon at short leg and asked: 'Can you see anything there?'

And Boonie replied: 'Yeh. Terror.'

When Boonie was hit flush on the chin by a bouncer from Patrick Patterson on his way to a Test century in Jamaica, he accepted a few running repairs and afterwards had stitches inserted in a nasty gash — without any anaesthetic! The West Indies knew what they were up against and didn't bother with much sledging when Boonie was at the receiving end. And they often had to re-think their strategy against the little man from Tasmania because they knew a series of bouncers would get them nowhere. Against Boonie, it was futile.

Boonie was held in high regard and affection by the Australian public, but I doubt if they actually appreciated just how important he was to the rebirth of the side. I was disappointed when the selectors lost faith in him, and delighted when he said he would play on with Tasmania following his retirement from international cricket, at the end of the 1995–96 Test series against Sri Lanka. I know he still has a great contribution to make. Too many players drop out of the game when their international careers end, instead of putting something back. I remember how much I enjoyed the years I spent playing grade cricket after my retirement in 1968 and am sure David will enjoy playing on with Tasmania for at least a couple of years to come. He is the sort of bloke who will always enjoy playing the game and I have no doubt it will do a hell of a lot for Tasmanian cricket to have his experience and influence on tap.

He also plays a mean game of golf and, no doubt, will now concentrate on getting meaner. Don't let the style fool you; he may look a bit like a threshing machine but he gets results. He plays off eight or thereabouts, as I remember. If you play him for money make sure the stakes are not too high. Boonie the golfer, like the cricketer, like the man, just never knows when he's beaten.

THE late Kenny Barrington is probably the most successful England batsman since the war and in many ways the most underrated. I am biased, because I became a close friend of Ken and because I rate so highly quality, guts, attitude and all the things which the Barringtons and so many of the genuine cricketers of the world stand for. Look at his record against Australia, in particular, and tell me why he never achieved the lasting fame he obviously deserved. Wally Grout once remarked: 'Whenever I saw Ken coming to the wicket I thought a Union Jack was trailing behind him.'

On many occasions Ken carried the weight of England's chances on his shoulders. Yet he was good enough to finish with a Test average of 58.67. In England he played 13 Ashes Tests and scored 1065 runs at an average of 59.16. In Australia he played 10 Tests and made 1046 at 69.73. The players of a generation pitted against him admired and respected a real competitor, a true Englishman who fought for his country as hard as they fought for theirs and then smiled his broken smile over a beer afterwards. It has always seemed to me that he never received the recognition he deserved.

Part of that was probably because of his adopted style of batting, which was admittedly very unglamorous, and his perceived slowness at the crease. He was even dropped by England for batting too slowly after making 137 against New Zealand, perhaps because England were expected to wallop New Zealand in the 1960s and Ken's seven and a half hours for 137 was too much to take. Couldn't they could do with that sort of stickability now! And simply rattling off the bare statistics of a long innings is deceptive, especially across the generations.

When I made 311 at Manchester in 1964 to secure the Ashes it was considered ultra-slow. However, it is usual for batsmen who make 200 these days to take longer getting there than I did on my way to the triple century. Times and expectations change. One reason for that, of course, is that batsmen nowadays don't receive as many deliveries in an hour as we did, but history does show that so-called attacking players were often not as quick-scoring as their image suggests. A pleasing style often gives a false impression of speed — and poor Ken certainly couldn't lay claim to that.

Ironically enough, he was a thrasher when he began with Surrey in the English county championship, a batsman who went after everything he could reach. While it worked he was praised, but when the same flashing stroke got him out he was accused of irresponsibility and inconsistency. So he changed his approach and became a really tough customer to remove. He opened his stance so that sometimes his left shoulder pointed in the direction of midwicket. Consequently, he always looked as though he would be easy meat for an inswinger — but he never was. Even Alan Davidson, the greatest left-arm swing bowler of them all, found him hard to dislodge. Ken's wide-open stance, and method of playing back and across should have left him as a lay-down misère for a bowler of Davo's class — but Ken's record says otherwise.

Sometimes he would show glimpses of his old attacking self. Then he could be quite devastating, a great hooker in the short-arm jab mould and a wonderful square-cutter of the ball. Such an open stance meant he needed the ball really well up, rather than just slightly overpitched, but he was still able to smash it through the off-side. Being a leg-spinner himself — and always ready to talk about the art — he was a very competent player of leg spin, whereas most English batsmen have no idea. He may well have been the first English leg-spinner to learn how to bowl a flipper, after picking it up from Richie Benaud on a Ron Roberts tour to South Africa and Rhodesia in 1959. We Australians virtually adopted Ken on that tour. I think he liked our egalitarian approach to the game... and he repaid us by scoring more Test runs against us than any other batsman of the time!

His image as a dour man at the crease was nothing like the Barrington the players knew off it. Always good for a laugh, a great practical joker and impersonator and a wonderful mangler of the language. According to Ken, target shooters used 'high philosophy bullets'. He woke one morning having 'slept like a lark'. And he described the players at a buffet in Pakistan as 'a swarm of lotuses'. He loved brass bands and would take up the baton at the drop of a baton. And he had high ideals about the game he loved, one of a few players prepared to come out publicly against the highly controversial bowling action of Charlie Griffith when the topic was political dynamite in the mid-1960s. That issue took a lot out of Ken emotionally, but he felt an important principle was at stake.

Ken had a mild heart attack during the double-wicket tournament in Australia in 1968, after which he announced his retirement from first-class cricket. However, he stayed involved in top-class cricket as manager of England tours. He was assistant manager in Barbados in 1981 when he suffered a second heart attack and died in the arms of his wife Ann. It says a lot for the respect in which he was held that the ultra-competitive Fleet Street contingent on tour agreed to a man to delay the news of his death until it had been broken to his son, Guy, at boarding school.

Kenny Barrington, the player, had a well-developed technique which might not have suited every batsman but certainly worked for him. He had courage, enormous tenacity, integrity. He was a worrier who loved to chat between overs on the field, but once we discovered that we made sure he had nobody to talk to. I loved the bloke but gave instructions: 'Don't let's make Kenny feel too much at home.' Not that it seemed to affect him. Kenny, wrapped in his Union Jack, knew just what we were doing.

JAVED Miandad may have been the most scheming and irritating player ever to make an artform out of international batting. He was probably the most disliked player of his time in many respects — yet he was also the finest run-maker in all forms of cricket for many years. And that at a time when the game was full of class batsmen, an era in which great players like Greg Chappell and Viv Richards set the standards. Miandad made a cottage industry of rubbing his opponents and even some of his team-mates up the wrong way and that is an image which tends to overshadow his talents as a player. However, those who like him least rarely challenge his status as a batsman. He was quite exceptional.

The most vivid image Australians have of Miandad might well be from Perth in late 1981, when he and Dennis Lillee clashed very publicly in one of Test cricket's shabbiest incidents. The pair gently collided while Miandad was running through for a single, and Dennis responded by giving his opponent a little kick. With that, the Pakistani spun around, bat flourished above his head, and for a moment it seemed an awful, ugly clash was going to occur. I thought

Dennis was out of order that day, but he was not the only one. It was significant, though, that whereas Dennis snapped after a period of backchat both ways, Miandad never did. I do not think Miandad lost control for one moment during the incident; he was too calculating for that. He enjoyed pushing opponents to the brink and if they fell over, it was a victory he enjoyed with a quiet smirk. Gamesmanship was very much part of Miandad's make-up and remember that as well as making headlines and a profound nuisance of himself, he also made 79 in that Perth innings. Nobody should do what Dennis did that day, but if there was a deserving case for such an outburst, Miandad was probably it.

In Pakistan, Miandad took his antics as far as he could. He would perch at short leg and brandishing the ball every time he stopped it, as though he had taken a bat-pad catch. Against Australia in Lahore in 1988, Miandad appealed alone for a catch behind, then gave his slips cordon a public roasting for not joining in. Sure enough, next ball they all went up for something, anything. Typically Miandad. He was the most irritating man in the world.

But he could play, absolutely no doubt about that. In a sense, you knew just where he was coming from, and what to expect from him. Miandad had an up-front roguishness which was not entirely unattractive and I liked him for it. I saw his brinkmanship as an extension of his passion for his country; he was a streetfighter who knew the game in Pakistan was a political one and learned at a very early age that winning was everything. He had tremendous spirit and any game was fair game to him as long as they beat the opposition. If you nailed him, told him he was going too far and you'd bloody well do something about it, he would grin and wobble his head as if to say: 'Okay. Fair cop. Can't blame me for trying.' That probably made him more irritating than ever.

Behind the cheek and provocation, there was a superb batsman with an outstanding technique. Nobody in my long experience has watched the ball more closely or played it later than he did, a skill which came into its own on turning pitches. The Australia v Pakistan Test match in Karachi in 1988 was played on one of the worst pitches ever cooked up for an international match. It was an absolute shocker and we said so, and in many respects the Test was a sham. But Miandad made 211. He did get some help in so far as it seemed that he never looked in danger of being given out lbw, but credit where it is due, he never really looked as though batting on a such bad pitch was a complicated business. His ability to place the ball — a nudge here, a nudge there — was quite phenomenal and typical of his skills, while his skill in being able to play the ball so late drove our bowlers to distraction; they thought they had beaten him, half-way to throwing up their arms in triumph when he clipped one round the corner for a couple. And he'd take off with a little grin, all the happier for knowing he was annoying them.

Technique was the key, so finely tuned that he was able to fit perfectly into one-day cricket when that became the world fashion. I have always maintained that technically sound players will play any form of cricket well and Miandad was a brilliant example: a great Test player *and* one of the finest one-day players in the world. He might not have hit the ball as hard as some in the one-day stuff, but he could steer and place it intuitively, play very few dot-balls and hit over the top if that was required. He could improvise, which made life hard for opposing bowlers and captains, knew as the ball left his bat where he was going and whether the stroke was worth a single or two, and ran as well between the wickets as anybody in the game.

Miandad's record in Pakistan was probably cheapened by the suspicion that the lbw rule was suspended whenever he batted. When we arrived there in 1988, he had been given out lbw just three times in his previous 61 innings at home, spanning 43 Tests! It did not take long to figure out why. However, he scored runs in every country he played in and against every type of bowling and that is a mark of true class. Whether he was taking it up to the world's fastest bowlers or battling for national pride in crunch matches against India, Miandad absorbed the pressure and showed the highest class. He also survived and probably exploited the endless politics which infest cricket in Pakistan, no mean feat in itself in a career which began when he was only 18. The public will probably remember the great all-rounder, Imran Khan, as the quality Pakistani player of the modern era. I reckon the players will opt for Miandad.

LARRY Gomes must have felt uncomfortably like 'Larry Who' during his career with a star-studded West Indies side. It might not be pushing things too far to say that he was the only ordinary player in a team of celebrities during the late 1970s and early 1980s. Larry was the odd man out, the ugly duckling if you like, the one player who was never talked about in world-class terms. Yet his contribution to West Indian cricket, and to what made his side the best in the world, was invaluable.

When I first saw Gomes play, I made a hasty assessment of his ability, but then revised it with every pragmatic run he scored. The Australian team which toured the Caribbean in 1978 was without those players who had signed for WSC, but the West Indies played their 'Packer' men for the first two Tests of the series. During the early days of the tour, as the conjecture over whether the WSC men would play for the home side raged, it was inevitable that we would assess what their strength would be if the 'rebel' stars weren't around. Gomes played against us for Trinidad and my initial reaction was that here was a country bumpkin and that West Indian cricket couldn't be that strong if a bloke like him could make it into the Trinidad side. Sixty or 70 runs later, I thought differently.

His style was undistinguished, a bit unorthodox, and he was slightly built where so many West Indians were powerful. Put simply, there was nothing about him which suggested anything out of the ordinary. However, he had a great ability to put the bat on the ball, guard his stumps and accumulate runs. And he kept on showing this throughout a career in which he always played second fiddle to the stars in the side, always dug West Indies out of a hole when he had to, and always frustrated bowlers who thought he would be relatively easy pickings in a side jammed with so many power batsmen.

I would be hard pressed to remember a shot Larry played and describing his style is no easier. He had a minimal backswing, invariably worked the ball through the on-side from a line on the off stump and never ever played the ball with the full face of the bat. This was not the sort of foundation you would expect to build an international career on. And not the sort of stuff that commands full-page pictures in the ACB coaching manual. Yet he was mightily effective and in a team of dashers, his ability to shore up the middle order was a godsend. The West Indies might not have been in crisis very often in those days, but when they were, Gomes was usually the man who resolved it with a gritty and unglamorous innings which might well have been forgotten by the time the rehabilitation was complete and the Windies were in a position to bowl to another victory. Then it was the bowlers who grabbed all the plaudits.

Gomes' range was very limited — the twitch to leg, the odd cover drive, some slides down through gully and a sort of hook. But he was a devil of a bloke to bowl at because if you tempted him with anything wide he left it alone and if you bowled off-stump line he worked it away on the leg side. If you do not have the perfect technique — and that was Larry all the way — then the next best thing is the ability to watch the ball onto the bat. Get your head over the line, watch the ball onto the bat and you can get away with murder. Larry did not have a technique to take him far but he had obviously mastered that. He never gave up, rarely went outside what he knew he could do, and built an enviable career on very little. I admire him for that. At first sight, it was incongruous that he should make the West Indies one-day side, given their wealth of explosive batsmen. But every team of dashers needs a steadying influence, just in case, and he was the perfect foil, the perfect team man who would rotate the strike in favour of the bigger guns, pick off his own runs with a doggedness which drove bowlers silly, and often derailed a rival team's bowling plan.

His value in a team of strokemakers was enormous and a player of his type is clearly missed by the Windies now, with nobody in mid-order briefed to hold the innings together, keep it tight and frustrate the opposition when things go wrong. Larry Gomes had a fine grasp of what he could contribute to the side; perhaps inevitably, given the charisma of so many fine players around him, he was underrated during his career and will be undervalued by histories of the game. But not by those who played against him.

 WHATEVER A POTENTIAL INTERNATIONAL PLAYER'S SKILLS, APTITUDES AND CAPACITY TO LEARN, HE WILL NEVER BECOME A REALLY GOOD PLAYER — MUCH LESS A GREAT ONE — UNLESS HIS ATTITUDE IS RIGHT. What does he want to get out of the game? He can talk about money or fame or half a dozen other things that might go with becoming a proficient cricketer, but he will never really succeed unless he has passion. All the best players have it. Simply being proficient doesn't make you a champion. Proficiency is admirable enough, but there has to be something that goes beyond that; there has to be a real desire to do well, a passion for the game and a passion to do well at it. All the modern techniques in motivation and all the speeches in the world won't inspire a player who can't inspire himself. There has to be a passion to achieve and a pride in performance. Champions are never 'justa' people. They are never 'just a batsman' or 'just a bowler'. The 'justas' of the world often miss out on a lot of opportunity — and champion cricketers very rarely do.

❯

STEVE Waugh was the best batsman in the world in 1995, when he took everything the West Indies could throw at him in the Caribbean and confirmed the depth of his skill and temperament. Today, Brian Lara and Sachin Tendulkar are usually referred to as the world's greatest batsmen and they are both wonderful players who can lift their game to exceptional heights. However, they have not shown Steve's consistency in all sorts of conditions over the past few years.

Steve Waugh is now a classic example of a players' player and it is to his credit that he has reached this point — because he has had to work really hard at his game to establish his place among the world's best. There was no problem with talent — Steve has always had plenty of that — but there were flaws in his game which, unchecked, could have threatened his international career. Cricket is littered with great natural players who did not make it because they lacked the brain, the common sense or the application to make the most of their gifts. Fortunately for him and Australia, Steve has the brains to match his outstanding talents.

In his early days Steve was a purely instinctive player, thrilling to watch as he unleashed a string of breathtaking strokes and ultimately frustrating when he fell attempting shots which just weren't on. He was a classic example of the player with bags of natural talent who had not taken the trouble to couple it with technique. There is no point in having all the talent in the world if you are sitting back in the pavilion.

I first met Steve and Mark Waugh when I was appointed coach of NSW in 1984 and was immediately struck by their natural talent — and fascinated by their contrasting personalities, build and style. They share a huge talent for the game but otherwise there is not much identical about the Waugh twins. They had always been highly successful at whatever sport they tackled, but, at 19, Steve produced a little bit more than Mark and made the State team first.

Stephen hit the ball amazingly hard in those days, but it was obvious that he had a few technical problems — particularly a lack of flexibility in his knees. Steve played with very stiff knees, which meant he could not take a full step forward and could not get his eye-line right over the ball. He couldn't 'smell it out', as the old timers used to say. So he tended to drive with his weight on the back foot, which meant he often lifted the ball into the air or invited trouble from edges into the slips. However, once the problem was identified, Steve worked really hard at correcting it, though it took a long time, as long as four years, before he made a major contribution to Australian Test cricket.

He was too gifted a player to waste and no sound judge doubted he would establish himself in a big way. And there had been frequent glimpses of his class, as in our 1987 World Cup win, but he did not really pull it all together as a batsman until the 1989 Ashes tour. Steve began that series with scores of 177 not out and 152 not out in the first two matches. He played some magnificent shots, and there are wonderful pictures of him playing forward with his back knee actually on the ground; the sort of stuff they put in coaching manuals. How's that for flexibility!

Steve still has problems occasionally, even today, but nothing he cannot handle; he was, and is, an example of a player with exceptional talent who needs the nuts and bolts of technique to put it to full use.

Steve was rushed into the NSW and Australian sides probably a bit before he was ready, certainly in terms of his batting. But he had huge talent and the Australian scene were not overburdened with that at the time. He was too good to miss. For a period, his bowling kept him in the Australian side. He was always experimenting, always trying something new and unexpected. He and Simon O'Donnell really became engrossed with innovations, which in Steve's case included the perfection of a leg-break. This was no mean feat for a man who bowled quicker than most batsmen expected. He varied his pace, made the leggie drop suddenly and was never afraid to innovate, even in pressure situations. Batsmen who just wanted to hit everything out of sight got into all sorts of embarrassing difficulties and nobody really worked out all his subtleties. I remember Viv Richards in Brisbane ducking under a slower ball which looked as though it had slipped out and would pass harmlessly over the stumps. But it dropped sharply and hit Viv in the middle of the back; the only bloke on the ground that day who thought it was not lbw was the umpire.

Steve is naturally aggressive as a cricketer and his bowling reflects that — quicker than it looks so that he can force batsmen onto the back foot, very accurate and with a wicked yorker. Put it all together and he is the hardest bowler to get away in international cricket.

As I mentioned earlier, after his triumphal Ashes tour in 1989, Steve hit problems against short-pitched deliveries. Nobody in his right mind likes facing bouncers and it is pure bravado to claim otherwise, but recognised batsmen have to learn to cope. Steve, typically, worked hard at strengthening his technique against the short stuff. He was occasionally taking his eye off the ball and thrusting his hands outwards, popping up catches down the leg side. As an old opener, I also felt he was watching the ball off the pitch rather than out of the bowler's hand and therefore costing himself precious time to frame his strokes. And his body was too side on. His toes pointed to point which did not allow him to glide the ball down the leg side or get inside the line. Steve worked on all those suggestions and the thought that it really does not matter how awkward a batsman looks as long as he survives. The knowledge that his technique was sound gave him confidence and by 1995 in the West Indies, and despite being subjected to an illegal amount of the short stuff, he was the best batsman around.

Steve played a lot of indoor cricket as a kid and that undoubtedly helped develop his fielding ability. The indoor game is played in restricted space, the need for run-outs is paramount and fieldsmen develop a quickness of mind and hand. You can see it when Steve flicks the ball through his legs or round his body or attempts the impossible return to the stumps. He has won run-outs at the non-striker's end by deliberately putting just one finger to the ball on his follow-through. Deliberately, mind you. A very quick brain. He has lost a bit of pace now, but not his inventiveness and therefore not his ability to take wickets. And when you add together all his qualities, as a batsman, bowler and fielder, the result is a wonderfully formidable package.

CHAPTER 9

The decline of English cricket

The decline of English cricket is bad news for the game around the world. Don't get me wrong; I am perfectly happy to give the Poms a beating and, despite their failures in recent Test series, the Ashes tradition is still strong and important. I don't cry too many tears for professional players whose standards are unjustifiably low, but I do wonder how on earth England let it happen. With their resources and tradition they should be producing far better players than they are. At the moment they are obviously a bit of a 'basket case' which is sad. But it is also their own fault and it is worth taking a look at some of the factors in their decline, if only to avoid repeating them. I would much rather see Australia on top of a strong international circuit than a weak one.

The county system seems to have stuffed up badly. The overriding priority in English cricket is the welfare of the counties and while that is understandable, it is, in the interests of the overall game, a selfish, introverted view. The way cricket is structured now, profits flow down from the top, yet England have made too many decisions which mitigate directly against producing successful international cricketers. The county representatives who form the Test and County Cricket Board have messed about with the game looking for some formula to attract spectators, sponsors and cash to their own clubs. And the changes they have made over the last decade or so are cosmetic measures which have not only failed to lift standards, but have produced a whole generation of cricketers who think they are worlds better than they really are.

The proof of this is England's international record. The county game has opted for the quick fix, for changes in regulations to produce 'attractive' cricket rather than accomplished cricketers. An emphasis on creating results, as if the public really wants to see a mediocre team beat an ordinary one. The standard of Sheffield Shield cricket is miles higher than county cricket; this is indisputable and part of the reason is that it is a much tougher competition in which to earn a living. The Sheffield Shield does not attract the attendances it used to — although I'm convinced the public interest is still there — but the Australian administrators kept their nerve and preserved an atmosphere in which standards were important.

Groundsmen in the UK were at one point encouraged and even instructed to prepare 'result' pitches. They were supposed to seam or bounce or both. A couple of seasons later the fashion was for pitches which turned. There were quality controls of a sort, but unless a county produced an absolute 'homer' of a pitch designed to suit their particular bowling strengths — and many did — the chances were that Lord's would turn a blind eye. The inevitable consequence of this philosophy was that bowlers stopped learning to bowl. All they had to do was land the ball just short of a length and let the seam do the work for them, or turn the ball adequately on a pitch designed to make ordinary spinners look like world-beaters. And, to make matters worse, the administrators introduced cricket balls with big, ropey seams which took a piece out of the pitch and made every piddling medium-pacer in the land think he was a Test player. I could name 30 such bowlers, all of whom used to swagger in and be a real handful for county batsmen, simply because they dropped the ball somewhere around middle stump, which is really not that difficult, and let the pitch do the rest.

Bowlers lost the ability to bowl on good pitches — which is what Test pitches usually are — and the effect on the batsmen was just as bad. An attitude developed that it was impossible to last long, so batsmen might as well throw the bat, or at least go for their shots. It may have been superficially entertaining, just what the counties ordered, but it did nothing for the standard of cricketers who also had to compete at international level. In test matches, bowlers who had not mastered their craft and batsmen who did not know how to construct a long innings were found out. The better players looked like better players, of course, but the overall standard was exposed.

I remember back to Headingley, in 1989, when Australia were sent in by England captain David Gower. We built up a huge score and finally won a crucial victory on the final day, and afterwards Gower was roundly criticised in the media for his decision to bowl first. We thought this criticism was unfair, especially considering that we had seriously considered putting England in if we won the toss. Although we had finally decided against it, the pitch would have been beautiful to bowl on before lunch. However, England bowled atrociously and after the first break we had an absolute picnic.

Everybody wanted to rail against Gower's decision rather than the fact that the bowlers weren't up to it. Nobody seemed to heed the lesson. Next morning, before play recommenced, I went to look at the pitch and it was obvious that the red scuff marks where the ball had pitched were two metres short of where England should have been bowling. I called our bowlers over and told them: 'That's where England went wrong yesterday. We are not going to bowl there, we are going to bowl up there.' This situation was repeated more than once on that tour and it soon became obvious that English bowlers had lost their natural length; they generally bowled too short because they had been brought up on pitches designed, some would say doctored, to give them excessive help.

Batsmen who are not used to building a long innings can usually be worn down, quite quickly by international standards. In 1989, and again in 1993, we worked on the theory that if you kept it tight and made the English batsmen work, they would eventually make the mistake. These players still hit the bad ball as fluently as anybody in the world, but there are not enough of them temperamentally schooled to play long innings in Test cricket. I cannot emphasise this point enough: the counties wanted results, entertainment, cameo innings and a shallow sort of excitement to attract the crowds. They ignored the long-term view, thinking that has had a huge effect on their cricket.

I don't think the attitude of many county professionals does the game any favours either. As there are so many counties looking for players, the pool of talent is stretched thin. A high percentage of players at county level are not very good. And, worse than that, they show precious little evidence of wanting to be. Too many cricketers are content with doing the minimum, scoring just enough runs or taking enough wickets to make sure they get a renewed contract, without any real desire to improve their game above the level of county adequacy. Not every player is like that, of course, but a woefully high proportion are, which makes the better ones look even more superior.

The basic aim of most batsmen seems to be to cobble together 1000 runs a season, which in my opinion is an underachievement given the number of innings they play. Similarly, bowlers seem happy to aim for 50 wickets in a first-class season. This is a shocking attitude, especially when you consider that the life of a county cricketer is pretty desirable; the perks of being big fish in little ponds come with earnings that are comfortable, even at the lower end of the scale (without, I must admit, being huge).

Comfort seems to be what so many English professionals are all about these days. They are paid for what amounts to six months work on the county circuit and, while there are always complaints that they cannot find winter jobs and so on, surely even the most ordinary county cricketers develop enough contacts and enough exposure to set themselves up with employment outside the season? The bloke who won't extend himself during the cricket season is probably the one who cannot find a job in the northern winter — and then complains loudest about it.

 **THE AUSTRALIAN TEAM TAKES PRACTICE SERIOUSLY AND I THINK IT'S FAIR TO SAY THAT A LOT OF OUR DRILLS AND METHODS HAVE BECOME MODELS FOR THE REST OF THE WORLD. These practices** are usually noisy, with a good deal of chiacking and boisterousness. The blokes actually enjoy it and so they should, since it's going to be a very basic and familiar part of their lives in the game. If the practice routines and atmosphere are repetitive and boring, players soon lose interest and start going through the motions; we try to create a situation where practice is competitive in a good-natured sort of way. The top players prefer it that way and I'm sure kids do, too.

After all, any cricketer is going to spend 80 per cent of his time in the field and if he hates the practice side of it, he's not likely to enjoy himself too much during the real thing. We never talk about hard work, just valuable work that has to be done and therefore might as well be enjoyed. I tell the players that it's a real opportunity to show what they can do, to show off, if you like. Our practice sessions over the years became so intense and colourful that the crowds would come along early to see us at it — not just to watch a famous player bat or bowl in the nets, but to watch the team going through their pre-match drills. More than one opposition coach found our appetite for practice and training quite intimidating.

Top-level players face a very heavy workload these days and that has to be borne in mind when you devise a coaching framework. Players will always want the easy way out and cry that they are doing too much, but there is a lot of cricket being played and the balance between keeping players sharp and overworking them is a lot finer than it used to be. That's another reason why enjoyment and intensity are important. I would much rather have a taut two-hour session than a meandering three-hour one. Players get stuck in a lot more keenly, do the work and yet don't feel they are on the treadmill hour after hour between matches. **)**

England's system for bringing youngsters into the game could do with a real overhaul. In many counties, it simply doesn't seem to exist. Some have a long history of strong league competitions — although they are by no means as strong as they once were — but many seem to rely on picking up players where they can. During the two years that I was coach at Leicestershire, I studied the coaching structure right through the county and told the committee I did not think they could survive unless they encouraged and produced more young players. The response was that they had never had a history of producing their own players. 'We only have a population of one million,' I was told. Perth, the capital of Western Australia, had a similar population at the time and the West Aussies had been top dogs in Australian cricket for the best part of the previous 20 years. 'We have to get out there and give it a try,' I pleaded, but nothing was done.

To prove the club's point, I was shown a list of Leicestershire players through the years who were actually born in the county. There were perhaps 100, it seemed pathetically few. Yet the club seemed to think this fact justified their approach. Because little had been done in the past to produce local talent, it seemed little could be done now.

I enjoyed my time at Leicestershire, but there was plenty of opposition to my attitudes and methods. James Whitaker had toured with England representative sides and was regarded as one of Leicestershire's better players. 'The big problem with Bob,' he commented after my stint there was over, 'is that he wanted us all to be Test cricketers.' Well fancy that! Isn't that what everybody is supposed to aspire to? James probably meant that I wanted them all to work at their game as hard as Test cricketers. And I did.

Too many players accept the good life of county cricket without really stretching themselves. That attitude is going to be hard to change, however, because big money is coming through from television rights and the counties are beginning to feel quite well off again. In my opinion, a large part of the future of English cricket at the international level depends on how the counties are allowed to use their TV windfall: If they simply give mediocre players more money they will not lift standards and there will be precious little investment in the years to come. If the game's administrators are wise, though, they will dish the money out to the counties with strings attached — so much will have to be spent on junior development, so much on coaching. And the money will have to spent well.

England is very impressed with the success of the players who came through the Australian Cricket Academy in Adelaide and there is a strong push to establish a national academy in the UK. The West Indies, too, have been talking the same way for some years. In the case of England, I am sure this would be just another quick-fix solution. Simply setting up an academy is not going to solve England's cricket problems; they need to be tackled at the roots — in the schools and the league clubs, and at the counties themselves.

The young players who have got away are England's problem, not the lack of some sort of finishing school for the already-accomplished player. In simple terms, at present England have nothing to finish. The Australian Academy is a finishing school, an environment which can fast-track the education of the most promising young players and, as such, it is very useful indeed. However, it does not discover talent and is not designed to. The talent is discovered by a whole network of state and country associations; by the time players go to the Academy the majority have already played representative cricket. This is worth stressing, because the nature of the Academy in Adelaide is misunderstood whenever the Poms talk about establishing their own. They have this great vision of a bloke with his boots over his shoulder knocking on the door, being welcomed in, and then emerging from the Academy a year later as the new Fred Trueman or Frank Tyson. The Australian Academy cannot succeed without a network of leagues and talent identification and neither would a national one in England. It is a valuable part of the system, but the idea that Australia's best young players are 'products' of the Academy is a dangerous cliche. They are products of a solid Australian system.

When I first toured England, in 1961, there was still this extraordinary distinction between the amateur and professional — the gentleman and the player. And, although it seemed quite ridiculous to me in many ways, this arrangement probably did have distinct effects on the way the game was played. The county sides were invariably captained by an amateur and, to my surprise, most of the professionals wanted it that way. This, it seemed, was because the amateur did not rely on the game for his livelihood and could therefore afford to be more dashing, more cavalier, more devil-may-care. He could take the rap if things didn't work out. Certainly, a lot of the amateurs were the most attractive cricketers. Some, of course, were far duller and more negative than the dullest professional, but that's the way it goes. Most of them had a lightness of spirit which was good for the English game at the time.

The system was abandoned a year later, and the professionals immediately went about taking a lot of the fun out of the game. They talked about what hard work it was, and complained about their pay and conditions. They still do, and really, that is nonsense. Not many people in life have the opportunity to make sport their livelihood, to do for a living what others do for recreation. The list of English professionals over the past 30 years includes a number of truly superb players, but many others have had a skill for accentuating the drudgery rather than the free spirit of the game. This attitude struck me so forcibly that I refused to let any team I coached talk about hard work, even when it most certainly was. We are doing what we want to do, I would say, so let's enjoy it.

There was a fast bowler at Leicestershire who certainly had talent, but was a dreadfully hard man to get onto the field. I felt that, whatever his own ability, he did not give enough to the side, and did not help the people around him. There was not enough heart in what he was doing. One day his role in the side was being discussed — he did take wickets when the pitch was lively — and club officials, who obviously liked him, could not appreciate that his influence needed to go deeper than that. When they asked me why I criticised him, I pointed out of the window. Our fast bowler was wandering out to practise — with a cup of tea in his hand! Very English and, symbolically, very typical. That same player would tell anybody within earshot what a hard and miserable existence he led. He talked a tough life and wanted to live an easy one.

Years ago, the English system undoubtedly was a hard grind, not least because of the travelling involved — usually on narrow roads late at night with huge distances to be covered before the next match. In 1961, the Australian team received a memorable taste of what English players had to put up with as a matter of routine and it wasn't pleasant. We often arrived at our hotel at 2am on the day of a match. On one occasion, we left Hastings — and you can't get much further south than that — and ended up in Scarborough, in the far north of Yorkshire. The match at Hastings had finished at 4pm. We caught a bus to London, a train north, stopped in York for a bite of breakfast at the Railway Hotel, and then on to Scarborough, which we reached what seemed like half an hour before the match was due to start. That was an extreme case, but English county players often put up with something similar. They had cause for complaint then, but not the present county players, who are blessed with motorways and fast, sponsored cars. But they still like to talk as though nobody has a harder lifestyle. It is nonsense. And the fact that they complain about what they do is so often reflected in the way they do it. Their attitude is wrong.

Looking at what's wrong with English cricket nowadays, I can't help reflecting on the performances and influence of Ian Botham. Not that I blame him for a moment; he was a genius in his own way, a huge player in his time and frankly, more of an Australian than a Pom in his attitudes and approach to the game. However, Botham's wonderful years for England may have been counter-productive in the broadest sense. He carried his country so magnificently that the team's flaws were overlooked; everybody stood and applauded the man's ability to win matches on his own without ever questioning why such heroics were necessary. Botham papered over the cracks, and the establishment, whether they took to him or not, were only too willing to let him capture the headlines if it meant saving them from embarrassment.

During Botham's monumental Ashes series in 1981, when (either with bat or ball) he won three consecutive Test matches pretty much all by himself, England had far too many spare parts players. This was true not just of the national team, but also the county scene. While Botham dominated, the shallowness of English cricket was ignored. His team-mates so often became superfluous. It became a boast to say that Botham beat Australia on his own and when you consider he scored 399 runs and took 34 wickets — after doing next to nothing in the first two Tests — that is fair comment. The fact that so many players around him weren't good enough was forgotten. The English captain in the famous series, Mike Brearley, is probably the classic example — a man who developed a reputation as a top-line captain and can point to his record to prove it. However, Brearley was not a good enough batsman to hold down a place in a genuine Test side. And, as a captain, where would he have been without Botham?

As long as Botham could work miracles nobody looked for any deeper flaws. And in that respect — and with no disrespect to a player I admire immensely — Botham was bad for English cricket. It was certainly no fault of his, but the game grabbed his coat tails and hung on for too long. Long after he had ceased to be good enough, Botham was being trumpeted as the Messiah of the English game. In 1989, he was a shadow of his former self, and you did not have to be a genius to see that. Yet the Poms clung to the belief that they only had to unleash him on Australia and the Ashes were theirs. In all the ballyhoo, the only people who were unimpressed by the menace of Botham were those he was supposed to intimidate — the Australian team. We respected him, of course, but we did not see him as a bogeyman. I can see Botham now, attempting a huge slog but being bowled by our leggie, Trevor Hohns, for a duck in England's first innings of the fourth Test, at Old Trafford. In his glory days, Botham would not have tried to hit the ball so hard. It was sad to see a man finish like that when he had given so much to the game.

In the years between his great successes and decline, England had beaten Australia at home and in Australia, to strengthen the myth that everything in the English rose garden was, well, rosy. But Australia, itself, was struggling for much of this time. Fortunately, we saw the realities of this situation, learned lessons and embarked on a well-defined program to rehabilitate ourselves. Meanwhile, English cricket fiddled with its domestic competition and appeared to dismiss the consequences of planning only in the short term. England will win matches again. Everybody does. But for the moment, they are paying dearly for a lack of proper management over many years.

CHAPTER 10

Cup chaos

Two World Cups have been played on the Indian sub-continent and if money talks — and in sport today it often shouts its head off — there will be a strong push for many more major cricket tournaments to be taken to the sub-continent in the future. That, in itself, will be no bad thing, given that the spectators in India and Pakistan are among the most enthusiastic and knowledgeable cricket crowds in the world. They are not blase, they do not accept major cricket events as a right, they still show a real delight in seeing top players in their countries and they follow the game avidly through the media. They deserve the best.

However, none of these pluses will be a consideration if the sub-continent gets much more cricket exposure in the future. The bottom line is money. India is reputed to have the richest cricket board in the world and no wonder when you look at the potential profits (which are still relatively untapped) the massive, sports-mad population offers to world television. The Indian board is in a position to offer huge financial incentives to secure international tournaments and there is no doubt it does so without apology. There is nothing particularly wrong with that, provided that the interests of the game are never neglected. And there's the rub.

The World Cup of 1987 was superbly organised and went without a major hitch; we frankly expected the worst before we arrived but were happy to say that the tournament was a triumph. And not just because Australia won. The 1996 World Cup, on the other hand, was a severe letdown. It was bedevilled by problems, not all of them major, that were enough to take the edge off the occasion. One mosquito bite is a nuisance, a dozen become serious. The consensus of opinion was that the organisation of the last World Cup lost the plot. Profit became a bigger consideration than the game and the teams involved were messed about intolerably. And this is not merely the kind of whinge you have often heard from teams that tour the sub-continent but fail to handle the change in environment and culture; Australia were more than prepared for the so-called difficulties involved. But the way the teams, and the game, were treated must be borne in mind when the subject of international cricket, World Cups, and the Indian sub-continent are discussed in future.

Australia's preparation for the '96 World Cup began months before the event, with a series of meetings between our relatively-new captain Mark Taylor, our physiotherapist Errol Alcott and myself (as coach). We knew that winning back the Cup would be a tall order, but we also felt we had some advantages because we had won it when it was played in India and Pakistan nine years earlier and we'd recently made tours to Pakistan and Sri Lanka. Many of the players we would use had experienced playing in India and that would be an advantage because the culture shock of the sub-continent can be pretty disorientating to the unwary. Expect the unexpected, of course, and above all, stay healthy. There is not much point planning match tactics down to the last detail if the players who are supposed to execute them are unfit to play.

That is where Errol came in. He has been with the Australian team since 1984, making all the tours and facing much the same problems as the players themselves. He has vast experience and, apart from being a superb physio, also has a priceless practical knowledge of medicine. Errol is not a doctor, but his father is. Health was a very high priority in our discussions — how to avoid the pitfalls, what simple precautions to take, where to draw the line between sensible self-management and a whiff of paranoia which can overtake teams in very foreign parts.

Errol did his research and laid out a set of simple ground rules, the sort of common-sense stuff which any tourist might be advised to bear in mind. Eat only food which has been cooked, beware salads which look very tempting, but which may have been washed in dodgy water, and eat only the fruit which you have peeled yourself. An arm full of jabs and a bit of logic should see most players through, although we accepted we would get the odd case of 'Delhi belly'. But we never had a player so ill that he was not available for a match — and that was the point as far as we were concerned. Our attitude was not panic or paranoia, it was preparation.

The ready availability of bottled drinking water makes a huge difference, although the locals still think it's quite a lark to charge the visitors for water while they happily drink the stuff out of the local river! Mind you, it still pays to check the seal on bottle caps before opening them, while the health authorities ask you to destroy the plastic bottles after use because there's a growing trade in refilling bottles with water which has not been purified.

That's the sort of message we passed on to the players, together with a few philosophical points about visiting and playing on the sub-continent. It can be delightful and it can be totally frustrating. Some years ago, Jim Higgs took a photograph of a slogan painted on a house in Madras — 'To Lose Patience is to Lose the Battle' — and it was adopted by visiting Australian teams. Of course, this is easier said than done in many respects, but before the '96 tour the players were left in no doubt that whatever frustrations occurred they had to be met head-on, understood, tolerated and on no account allowed to divert them from what the tour was about: winning the Cup. The biggest discomfort likely to face the players was lack of breathing space; India is simply wall-to-wall people. The crowds at the matches would be huge and even the atmosphere on the streets can be positively claustrophobic. Australians are accustomed to their own space, but they would not get much of that on tour, where the crowds, anxious to say hello or shake hands or just touch their heroes, would press in on them. This is a compliment to the players, but not one they always handle easily; a sea of faces, however smiling, may be intimidating and can become quite frightening in some circumstances. It is their culture, their custom and their way of showing support and admiration. Although it may be irritating at times, you need to be prepared to handle it.

A lot of myths have arisen around touring the sub-continent, most of them not very complimentary. Stories about sub-standard accommodation, lack of hygiene and primitive facilities were probably true once — the early tourists undoubtedly did it pretty tough — but the modern hotels are as well-equipped as any in the world. The Taj group of hotels was official host to the tournament, so we knew we could look forward to very good accommodation, some of it quite splendid. In fact, the better hotels in metropolitan India rank among the best in the world.

Mind you, the old stories persist and are probably exaggerated — the toilet jokes, bugs in the bed, rats in the rafters. It is easy to look for problems. England seem particularly prone to treat the sub-continent like a trip off the end of the world; I read that one young man on a recent 'A' tour there even packed a suitcase full of tinned food! That is clearly going over the top, not just because it ignores the realities — there are four superb restaurants in the Taj Palace in Delhi, for example — but also because it reflects a hopeless attitude of mind. Dear Dickie Bird, the famous English umpire, made his first trip to India and Pakistan for the 1987 World Cup, practically boarded himself in his hotels and treated every scrap of local food as though it was a poisoned chalice. It was suggested that the first time he ventured out of the hotel foyer and into the daylight was to make his way to his first match. Dickie didn't escape a bit of stomach trouble and, even if he had, the whole trip must have been a nightmare for him. All because he went there with premonitions of doom.

We would, though, have our rat-in-the-room story to tell — in Chandigarh in India, when a meeting of the fast bowlers in Mark Taylor's room was interrupted by a fat specimen running out of the bathroom, up a wardrobe and into the ventilation shaft! By the time the tale has been recounted a dozen times it will involve at least a dozen rats as big as cats.

Keeping the players fit and in the right frame of mind were important, but the crux of our pre-tournament planning went straight to the heart of winning the trophy: which players did we want to take and what was our best strategy for success in the conditions we were likely to face? We talked over a number of options and possibilities, modifying this idea, accepting or discarding that. We had basically agreed on the best way of approaching the series. There was some discussion on the use of a thrasher to open the innings, a tactic which had been employed by various teams in the recent past in an attempt to take full advantage of the field being inside the circle for the first 15 overs. I didn't like it, never have. It was agreed that the format we had developed and which had served us well in the past was a better option — use a batsman with proven skills rather than a slogger who would be a hit-and-miss merchant.

We knew from experience that the biggest innings are built on a solid base, not the crossed-fingers approach of a windmill hitter who may get 50 or may get out next ball. Players with the skill and experience to create an innings, capable of reading the game and accelerating sensibly, were what we had built our success on. As long as it continued to work, we saw no reason to change it. We wanted strokemakers in the squad, good runners between the wickets and a strong batsman in the mid-order who could consolidate the innings in the event of a collapse and push the score along when the circumstances demanded that. In Steve Waugh, we believed we had the ideal dual-purpose player. In fact, our approach to the batting component of the squad wasn't far different from the attitude we take to Test matches. Why should it be? Somebody would miss out and be unfortunate not to be chosen, but, in a limited squad, that is always the way.

As far as the bowlers were concerned, we wanted quicker bowlers who could swing the ball and spinners with the ability to vary flight and pace as well as give the ball a tweak. That formula was dictated by local conditions, where the pitches were likely to be a proverbial batsman's paradise. It went without saying that all the bowlers would have to be accurate, and they would need something extra to remain effective when the shine went off the ball or the pitches did not turn much. Damien Fleming had shown in Pakistan in 1994 that he could swing the ball and get top-order batsmen out, so he was very much in our thoughts when we began to stitch our plans together. And in Shane Warne, we had the world's best spin bowler, arguably the world's best bowler full stop. He was going to be the linchpin of the attack.

Our fielding philosophies were tried and tested; nobody was likely to win a place if he was a liability in the field. The emphasis would be on quick fieldsmen, who possessed the ability to take a direct line to the ball. There is a fashion for playing safe in limited-overs matches by circling the ball; we wanted fieldsmen who would attack it. Nobody in our side would give away runs by accompanying the ball into the outfield.

Our discussions on fielding highlighted the need to find somebody to replace Allan Border in the circle, but we all realised just how difficult that was going to be. What we were after was somebody who could knock the stumps out of the ground at both ends — and do it so regularly you never expected him to miss! A crucial position and hell of a man to follow; AB was the best fieldsman in the short midwicket area in the world.

We had a pretty good idea of the squad we wanted; the next step was to impress our ideas on the selectors, who would naturally have a few ideas of their own. We were fortunate in that we had established a very good understanding with the chairman, Trevor Hohns, and the rest of the panel, two of whom, Peter Taylor and Geoff Marsh, had been in the winning World Cup squad in 1987. These two especially knew just what we were up against and appreciated the special needs of the side. But, before the squad was finalised, there was the matter of a Test series against Sri Lanka at home.

We reckoned we would be the better team than the Sri Lankans in the Test series, but they would give us a real run for our money in the one-day series. And that's just what happened. What we did not expect was the amount of controversy that would be generated during the tour, or the way it would affect the relationship between the teams. Before the series, the feeling between Australia and Sri Lanka had been pretty good. There were occasional flare-ups, of course, but you get those in any sport. Fiery at the time, quickly forgotten and with no lasting harm done. This time, however, things seemed to go from bad to worse. Certainly, I have never known a series with more flashpoints — ball-tampering accusations, the no-balling of their off-spinner, Muthian Muralitharan, as a chucker, and heated exchanges between the players.

Our players were frustrated by the Sri Lankans' time-wasting tactics and really lost their cool in the second final of the World Series Cup. However, it would be wrong to paint the Aussies as the aggressors and the Sri Lankans as put-upon sportsmen suddenly confronted by a foreign culture. Sri Lanka have been playing international cricket for some time now and, let there be no mistake about it, they give as good as they get when it comes to the verbals and smart gamesmanship. They dine out on a reputation as the charming minnows of cricket, but only the naive really believe that; the fact is that Sri Lanka are as quick to cause trouble as they are to complain about it.

In many ways I don't blame them for that. World cricket is a tough school and they have to look after themselves. But I do wish they would not play the innocent at the end of the day. It is a form of hypocrisy which annoys the nations who play against them. There is nothing wrong in my book with a team standing up for itself; Australia did that in Pakistan in 1988 when we genuinely felt we were being wronged (and although we took some stick for our complaints then, I think sides touring Pakistan have profited from it). Once we had made our point, very forcibly, we got on with the tour and played it in the right spirit. Sri Lanka in Australia in 1995–96, though, seemed to think there was a conspiracy behind every decision in the series.

Awareness of the tempestuous political situation in Sri Lanka developed during the series and the issue of whether World Cup matches could be safely played in a country torn by civil war became a major talking point. The unpleasantness of the series in Australia led to all sorts of crank calls and letters being sent to members of the Australia team; Sri Lanka were obviously being represented back home as the injured party and that put immense pressure on the Australian players. Some received bomb threats, which are easy to dismiss as the work of a nut case when it is not your family involved, but deeply worrying to the people involved. The players might be able to put a brave face, but what about wives and children back home? What about the torment they must face? Whether to tour or not became an intensely personal problem for several players. We all knew that the threats came from a lunatic fringe who wouldn't actually carry them out. Or did we? Sports people are not supposed to go off

Mark Taylor on the 1989 Ashes tour, playing the hook shot. This shot disappeared from Mark's game for a while, but has returned as he tries to adopt a more aggressive attitude.

TOP: **Simon O'Donnell (left) and Peter Taylor — two of the best-ever Australian one-day bowlers.**
ABOVE: **In my opinion, Jeff Thomson's bowling action was technically perfect, straight out of the text-book.**

TOP: **Bruce Reid, my greatest disappointment. But for injury, he could have been anything.**
ABOVE: **Dean Jones, a 'one-off' cricketer, and definitely the best one-day batsman Australia's ever had.**

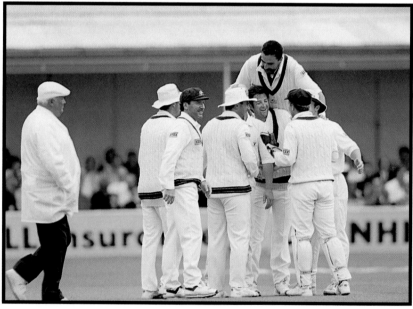

Merv Hughes was such a pest, but such a great man to have around. If you were a batsman, and you had to face Big Merv charging in (top) . . . no wonder he knew batsmen didn't want him around!

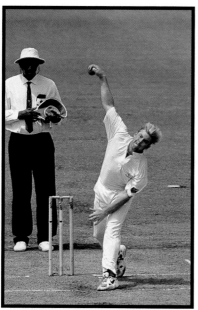

Three different views of Shane Warne, in the three different Tests, but in each he is, technically, perfect. Look at the balance, the wrist, absolutely beautiful.

THIS PAGE AND NEXT: **Four naturals and two self-made players.** TOP LEFT: **Michael Holding.**
TOP RIGHT: **Larry Gomes.** ABOVE: **David Gower.** OPPOSITE (TOP TO BOTTOM): **Javed Miandad, Aravinda de Silva, Sachin Tendulkar. What Gomes and Miandad lacked in pure natural talent they more than made up for through making the absolute most out of what gifts they had.**

Brian Lara — no small man should have this much power.

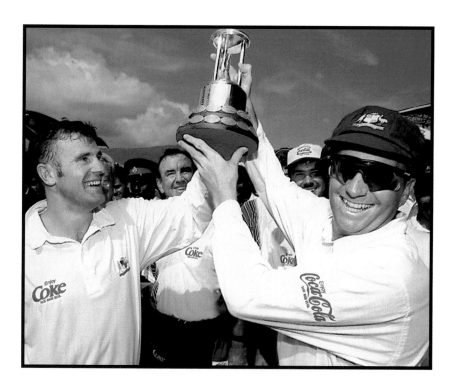

This is what makes it all worth while. TOP: **Mark Taylor (left) and Ian Healy with the Frank Worrell trophy after beating the West Indies in 1995.** ABOVE: **Mixing with the Sydney crowd after the tickertape parade that followed that triumphant tour.**

TOP: **The Australian team helps AB celebrate his new world run-scoring record in New Zealand in 1993. No-one deserved this more.** BOTTOM: **With scorer Mike Walsh in Calcutta at the start of our World Cup tour in 1996. At this point, we were having great difficulty finding a place to train, hence the antiquated facilities. Note also, the Black Cat commando, sub-machine gun and all, in the background.**

TOP: **Soon, though, we moved to Bombay, where we practised at the Gymkhana club, a magnificent relic of the Raj.** ABOVE: **A fielding drill in Vizag during the World Cup tour. It's not practice that makes perfect. It's *perfect* practice that makes perfect.**

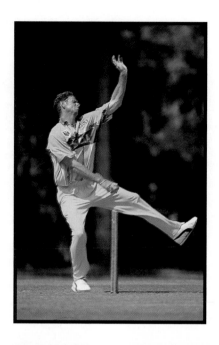

THIS PAGE AND NEXT: **Six members of the Australian World Cup squad. What strikes me about them is their similar physiques — the bowlers are all tall and wiry, rather than big and burly.**
TOP: **Paul Reiffel.** ABOVE LEFT: **Damien Fleming.** ABOVE RIGHT: **Glenn McGrath.**

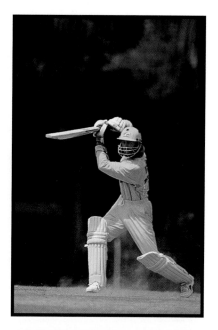

The batsmen are, in some cases, a little shorter, but just as superbly fit and athletic. TOP LEFT: **Ricky Ponting.** TOP RIGHT: **Michael Bevan.** ABOVE: **Stuart Law.**

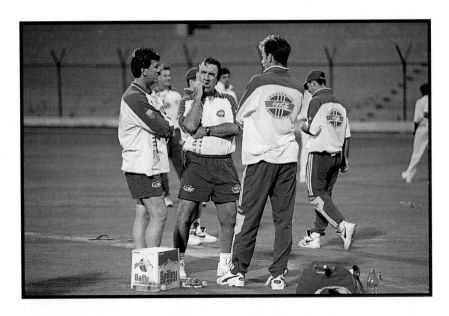

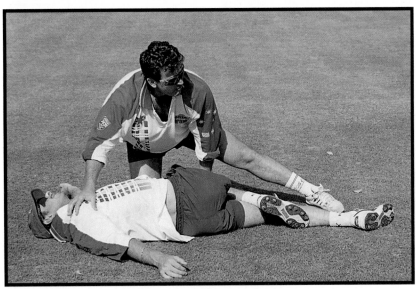

Of all the people involved in the Australian cricket team, few have been more valuable than physiotherapist Errol Alcott. His ability to get blokes back on the field and performing at their top is extraordinary. TOP: In conference with Paul Reiffel (right) and myself in Bombay. ABOVE: Getting Paul loose before the World Cup final in Lahore.

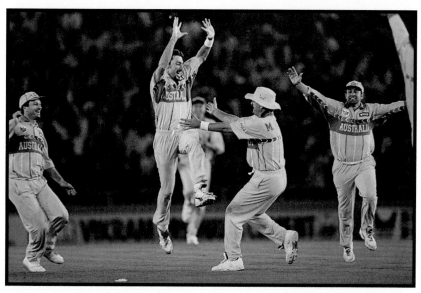

Two sides of the 1996 World Cup tour, and a tale of two semi-finals — the ever present security, this time in Calcutta, where the India–Sri Lanka semi-final was abandoned because of crowd trouble. And the celebrations in Chandigarh, after Australia had beaten the West Indies by five runs.

I've enjoyed a lifetime of cricket, and a decade as Australian coach . . . I wouldn't have changed a thing!

and fight wars. The consensus among the guys in the days leading up to the final Test of the series in Australia was that we wanted to play in the World Cup as organised, but what if?

Several meetings were held in the days before that Test in Adelaide, some of them attended by representatives of the Australian Cricket Board. The discussions were always frank and positive and the players were clearly aware of their responsibility to cricket worldwide. We were talking about one of the showpieces of international cricket, for heaven's sake, and the players were very conscious of that. I was very impressed by their sense of duty to the game, and by the balance they tried to strike between what they owed the game and what they owed themselves and, much more important, their families. They certainly weren't running scared.

During the Test, a meeting was held at which the players finally came to a conclusion. The issue had been kicked around in the media for ages: would they go to Sri Lanka or wouldn't they? It was not something they decided lightly, and the unanimous verdict was that they would accept the challenge and go. I thought it was a courageous decision, the sort that Australian teams have taken in the past without seeking too much credit and certainly without getting any. Australia was one of the first countries to visit Sri Lanka and then Pakistan during periods of civil unrest; we have not dodged the issue or the problems that go with domestic strife. Our players were personally unpopular in a country at war, yet they agreed to go there to play cricket. I think that takes guts.

What changed things was a bomb attack on buildings in the Sri Lanka capital, Colombo, which killed 80 people and established the awful fact that nobody could be declared safe, if they visited the city. The advice received from our political sources confirmed that the complexion of the conflict had changed and that they could not guarantee any sort of security. The idea that so-called terrorists would target military establishments only had obviously gone out the window. At this point, nobody really knew what would happen next.

The diplomatic wheels turned and the ACB were advised that touring was too risky. The Board acted on that advice and took the decision that the players would not go to Sri Lanka. It is hard to see what else they could have done in the circumstances. Soon afterwards, the West Indies Board did the same thing.

Suddenly, the air was thick with accusations of bad faith, even cowardice. The players began receiving abusive and threatening calls on a near-daily basis and a gaggle of Sri Lankan politicians went public with insulting and provocative statements which somehow suggested that living with terrorism was normal and anybody who did not accept it was a sissy. These criticisms and insults were hard for the players to take, not least because they had agreed to visit Sri Lanka and then been overruled, in the players' best interests, by the ACB. And, remember, Australia's record in helping Sri Lanka into international cricket was second to none. Sri Lanka was accepted as a full Test-playing nation in 1980 only after determined lobbying by the then chairman of the Australian Cricket Board, Fred Bennett. Fred had been asked to assess the state of Sri Lankan cricket when Australia stopped there en route to the Centenary Test at Lord's. He came down strongly in favour of Sri Lanka being given full Test status and eventually secured enough votes to beat some pretty entrenched opposition, much of it from England. Perhaps Sri Lanka's captain, Arjuna Ranatunga, should have remembered, before he started making silly statements, that without Australia's help he would not have had an internationally-recognised team to lead.

Another point which went unnoticed, but was not lost on the people involved, was that no insurance company was prepared to cover Australia in Sri Lanka. Insurance companies know a thing or two about acceptable risks. All the expert and dispassionate advice was not to go and, really, there was no alternative for the Board. Imagine the furore if they had sent the team to Sri Lanka and something dreadful had happened!

The decision not to go to Sri Lanka left a hole in our Cup preparations because we originally saw our time there as being the perfect way to acclimatise. Instead, we headed off to a training camp in Brisbane, not just because the practice facilities were top class, but because the weather would be hot, humid, and perhaps a bit uncomfortable for training. Just what we needed. Errol and I agreed that the priority in the first week on tour would be fitness; we knew we were a fit and energetic team already, but we wanted to improve on that so we would be ready for the hard environment in India and Pakistan. Conditions in Brisbane were perfect and for three days, the players worked as hard as any team I have ever seen — and that is saying a lot.

We also began to concentrate on what we saw as the specific difficulties of playing on the sub-continent and on areas where we had slipped a bit recently. Everybody had to get used to the idea of playing the game wet through; batsmen seem to change their gloves every five minutes and fielders are in a permanent lather. Expect it and it won't seem nearly as bad.

I had noticed that over a couple of years we had developed a bad habit of hitting too many shots at fieldsmen, instead of finding the gaps. So we put in some work on that. And our running between the wickets was not as sharp and aggressive as it could be, so I set up a session where we videoed all the players running between wickets and then analysed techniques and identified possible weaknesses. We had become a bit slack at pinching short singles, so I encouraged the players to bat with soft hands, drop the ball and go.

Another weakness which had crept into our game was a tendency to play too many dinky little shots — using half a bat to try and run the ball down to third man, playing across the line — all too clever by half. Those sort of shots have a high percentage of risk and the same result can be achieved by hitting the ball much straighter and through the gaps. We introduced a lot of variety into our fielding drills, with the overriding message: attack the ball, no circling. Grounds in India and Pakistan would be hard and rough, so fielders would not be able to wait for the ball, they had to get in and make the bounce work for them. We rehearsed underarm pick-ups and throwing at the stumps…

In fact, we concentrated on a great range of things that we had worked on before, all brought together in an intense training period which the players seemed to enjoy. They certainly responded positively enough. When we were not practising or training, the players formed discussion groups, asking questions and passing on tips about attitude, patience and pressure. Somebody remembered that the crowds are so noisy that it would probably be impossible to hear the captain at times, so everyone would need to watch for hand signals. And batsmen should develop good eye contact with their partners because it would be hard to hear calls. All little details, all important. Concerning the crowds, we stressed that Indian spectators know and love the game, and appreciate the good points of the team they do not support. But, for you or against you, they will make a devil of a noise. Prepare for fanaticism.

It struck us only a couple of days before we went to Brisbane that we were not entirely sure how we would actually be getting to the opening ceremony in Calcutta! We had asked PILCOM, the World Cup organising committee, for complete itineraries and hotel details months earlier and a list had duly arrived. But we were to discover bit by bit that it wasn't so much a schedule as a basis for negotiation. Three months earlier, the Australian Board had booked to fly to Sri Lanka and onwards with their official carrier, Cathay Pacific. Two weeks before the tournament PILCOM announced they would have an official Cup airline, but omitted to say who it was because negotiations were continuing. Eventually, it was revealed that Air India was the nominated carrier and we were expected to travel with them, which would have made a lot more sense had they offered more than a twice-weekly service to India, out of Perth. There we were, stuck in Brisbane with nowhere, apparently, to go. Until our Board took matters into their own hands and booked us on the shortest available route to Calcutta, via Bangkok, with Thai Airlines. No problems with the journey but the confusion was a nuisance, and an unnecessary hassle. And only the first of many.

Security can be a key turned in a lock, or a pensioner sitting on a chair outside a dressing room vetting visitors, or an army of police and commandoes bristling with weapons and briefed to squeeze every ounce of drama out of a World Cup. In Calcutta it was definitely the latter. If the number of bodies and rifles was a guarantee of safety, then every player in the tournament was immune from attack by anything below nuclear weapons. Security, sub-continent style, is manpower. We knew it would be extensive, but we didn't really appreciate the scale until we touched down in Calcutta on February 10. It was all of 20 metres from the aircraft steps to the waiting bus and as we were hustled on board we were surrounded by the security forces. Blackened windows, guards riding shotgun. Welcome to India.

I heard a security man direct the driver to the Oberoi Grand Hotel and pointed out that we were supposed to stay at the Taj Bengal. Not any more, we weren't; the run-around had already begun. From this point on, we might stay at the hotel originally designated by PILCOM and we might not. Throughout the tour, we were never absolutely sure, an experience shared by most of the competing nations. Not that we minded being switched to the Oberoi Grand; it is a fine hotel and the one from which we won the World Cup in 1987. Perhaps, we thought, it was a good omen in disguise.

We rather thought that our arrival would be a low-key affair, with a subtle police escort whisking us away as undramatically as possible. Instead it looked as though many millions of people had been given notice of our arrival. The streets were lined 10 deep, with cricket fans waving and cheering us on. Australia were the local favourites when we beat England to win the World Cup at Eden Gardens in 1987, and it was clear, nine years later, that they had not forgotten us. The bus inched its way through the crowded streets until it became ensnared in a monster traffic jam, as the crowds pressed against the bus and tried to get a glimpse of the team. The security men had no hope of keeping them at a distance and while the reception was wonderful in many respects it was also a disaster from a strict security sense. We certainly weren't living in fear of our lives, but it was obvious, right from the start, that the security forces' ability to control the crowds was strictly limited. Trying to outnumber this number of people is a bit of a waste of time. The boys were struck by the warmth of their reception and enjoyed the journey, but it was immediately obvious that they would be vulnerable to anything resembling a serious threat. For all the very visible security measures, that was going to be a fact of life.

As it turned out, the 250-room Taj Bengal hotel housed only the host nation players and about one million officials. Consequently, several of the so-called smaller teams had found themselves diverted to 'lesser' hotels, much to the disgust of a nation such as Zimbabwe. Zimbabwe's role at a meeting of the International Cricket Conference in 1993 was crucial in awarding the Cup to the sub-continent, after it had originally been agreed to hold it in England. Australia, New Zealand, the West Indies and South Africa supported England, but India, Sri Lanka and Pakistan did not and Zimbabwe was one country which gave them their support. Apparently, a number of 'associate' members of the ICC were offered big money to back the sub-continent bid and the tournament venue was changed, but I wonder what might have happened if Zimbabwe had known that, when it came to the actual event, they were going to be treated like second-class citizens.

There was more hard talking at the top level, when PILCOM and the ICC met to discuss the penalties which Australia and West Indies would face for their refusal to go to Sri Lanka. As usual, there was some pretty hysterical stuff and the Australian representatives at the meeting, Malcolm Gray and Bob Cowper, came in for a lot of stick. According to those who were there, the treatment of Gray and Cowper was a disgrace. It was, I am told, very personal and very offensive. PILCOM seemed determined to either force Australia and West Indies to play in Sri Lanka or extract huge fines instead. After two days' haggling most representatives apparently thought the penalty had been set and that the two countries would forfeit one point. Then there was another meeting and the penalty was raised to two. Interestingly, not everybody attended that second meeting; the organisation cannot have been too flash.

On the eve of the tournament, there was a meeting attended by every country in the Cup — captains, managers, coaches plus umpires and referees — which turned out to be an absolute bunfight. The meeting was chaired by Jagmohan Dalmiya, the convenor-secretary of PILCOM, and he became increasingly agitated at the number and breadth of questions which came from the floor. There were a lot of points still unanswered but Mr Dalmiya seemed to regard such questions as a reflection on the organising ability of his committee. In the sense that they needed to be asked, I suppose they were. Wes Hall had a distinguished playing career with West Indies and has been involved in administration — and politics — for many years. He is nobody's fool and was obviously appalled at the lack of information coming from the PILCOM side. At this meeting, he became very animated, to put it politely, and I can't say I blame him. It was a thoroughly unpleasant episode which achieved next to nothing and, by the time it broke up, it was clear that most competing countries were far from satisfied with the organisation of the event.

The opening ceremony did not exactly soothe anybody's forebodings. Not to put too fine a point on it, the expected extravaganza on a huge stage at the Eden Gardens stadium turned into a total stuff-up. The inquests went on for days afterwards, and the man who copped most of the criticism was one Gianfranco Lunetta, an Italian who apparently masterminded the whole show. He replied with a long, rambling letter to the Asian *Age* newspaper, but by then millions of people had seen the gruesome result — an event when just about everything that can go wrong did go wrong.

Overblown opening ceremonies at major sporting occasions seem to be a matter of the national pride of the host country these days and obviously they take an awful lot of arranging. Just how much is never more obvious than when the whole thing backfires and the Eden Gardens ceremony had everything — a bumbling announcer who welcomed Zimbabwe as South Africa, a laser show which had to be repeated twice in a desperate attempt to make sense of it. And a fireworks display in the middle of everything else. The players from 12 countries were arranged in a semicircle around the stage which meant nobody in the crowd could see all of them — as if the players mattered anyway — and the opportunity to show off some of the region's rich culture was entirely wasted. That was probably the worst aspect of the whole fiasco — the fact that local character was totally ignored in favour of a (supposedly) futuristic laser show.

The players would probably have welcomed the chance to walk round the ground and acknowledge the crowd. Instead they had to endure the whole thing, try to keep a straight face, and wonder what effect this giant stage was going to have on the cricket pitch beneath it, which was due to have a World Cup semi-final played on it in three weeks time.

CHAPTER 11

C an you believe that just 12 days before Australia's first match of the 1996 World Cup, nobody really seemed to know what to do with us? Our attempts to find out met with shrugs and evasion, so we eventually had to take matters into our own hands to some extent. For two days after the opening ceremony, we practised at a club in Calcutta, where the shortcomings of the facilities were compensated by the willingness of the local members to help out. They really could not have been more obliging and, since we still had an accent on physical hard work, the days certainly weren't wasted.

Unfortunately, though, the atmosphere in Calcutta was on the oppressive side, so we contacted the Gymkhana club in Bombay to see if they could arrange some practice facilities for us. The club has looked after visiting international teams in the past and has a high reputation. Luckily, they were happy to help so we embarked on another Indian adventure. First, the early morning flight from Calcutta was delayed. Then, most of the hotels in Bombay seemed to be packed out. But we got into one at Juhu Beach, which is about eight kilometres from the airport and 20 kilometres from the Gymkhana club. We enjoyed a quick lunch, then set off by coach for the club, a trip which took around 90 minutes. We practised for about three hours and learned, while we were there, that there was room at the Oberoi Hotel, which is much closer to the Gymkhana.

A quick decision was made to move hotels. Back we went to Juhu Beach (two-and-a-half hours in the traffic this time), to repack, then back into the city. By the time we booked in at the Oberoi it was around 10.30pm; we had left our hotel in Calcutta around dawn that morning. It had been a long day, but the decision to base ourselves temporarily at the Gymkhana club was undoubtedly the right one, as the facilities were splendid, the welcome warm and the few days we spent there an absolute delight.

We finished our week there with a match involving all our players and some locals. One of the guest players was Rohan, son of the mighty Sunil Gavaskar, who did not actually bat in the match but who is, by all accounts, a very accomplished player. The only cloud for us was a calf strain suffered by Craig McDermott; it didn't look too serious at first but unfortunately it was to cost Craig his place in the touring party.

Finally, after what seemed like an eternity of changing hotels and traipsing about, our tournament got under way. The venue was Visakhapatnam, down the coast from Calcutta, and a small city, as they say in India, with a population of less than two million. We knew very little about the place, except that it is mercifully known as Vizag, but it looked prosperous enough with hotels springing up round the city and a thriving port operation which is the eastern headquarters of the Indian Navy. The ground itself looked a bit underdone at first glance, but it proved pretty good, even if the outfield was a bit rough. There was nothing unusual in that. The practice pitches and facilities, though, were splendid and after two days' work we felt the batsmen were ready to go. And it turned out that way, against Kenya, one of the minnows of the tournament and pretty much an unknown quantity.

Playing teams like Kenya is never easy; Australia were expected to win, of course, so a victory would be routine while a defeat would be sensational. But upsets do happen in one-day cricket. Kenya were to beat the West Indies later in the competition, a result heralded by many as the philosophical high-point of the whole World Cup; everybody loves the David and Goliath contest when David wins. From a world cricket point of view, it was wonderful to see the way Kenya approached their matches and the sheer delight of their win over West Indies. I'm just glad it wasn't us they defeated.

They certainly had a go and it was amazing to see what they have achieved with relatively few players to choose from. Cricket in Kenya centres on Nairobi, with a few teams in Mombasa; it was encouraged by irregular international contact over the years and Kenya became an associate member of the ICC in 1981. The most important developments in the past decade have been the adoption of turf pitches and the emergence of local Kenyan cricketers, which reduced their reliance on imported Indian and Pakistani players. Kenya qualified for the World Cup by reaching the final of the ICC trophy, which they hosted in Nairobi, and then accelerated their World Cup preparations with a series of tournaments abroad and against strong touring teams.

Enthusiasm is essential, but it achieves only so much; when they played against us, Kenya looked like a side with genuine talent and potential and their other World Cup matches bore that out. It was their bad luck that they struck the Waugh twins in good first-up form. Mark made an impressive 130 and Steve contributed 82, after Kenya had whipped out Mark Taylor and Ricky Ponting early on. Their stand of 207, the highest for any wicket in World Cup history, lifted Australia to a powerful total of 304. There was no way we would lose from there if we bowled properly and the result was never in doubt despite admirable innings from wicketkeeper Kennedy Otieno and captain Maurice Odumbe. Otieno made 82, retired with severe cramps, and came back to add just three more runs before Glenn McGrath bowled him; Odumbe made 50 and really did play well on a good batting pitch.

The ability to defend a vulnerable total is one of the signs of a well-organised team in one-day cricket, especially when the opposition's most menacing player is in top form. So our 16-run win over India in Bombay — or should I say Mumbai — was particularly satisfying. We made 258, after at one stage looking as if we would make more — Mark Waugh and Mark Taylor put on 103 for the first wicket in 21.5 overs — then India were in obvious trouble when they lost 3–17. Sachin Tendulkar, though, played sparkling shots with the air of a man who has nothing to lose and a couple of frantic partnerships threatened to turn the game around. First, Tendulkar and Sanjay Manjrekar put on 73 in 12 overs and then Manjrekar and Nayan Mongia thumped 50 off 8.4. But the bowlers stuck at it despite some rough treatment and, in the end, Damien Fleming finished with 5–36 off nine overs to hold the line.

Shane Warne stepped up to take 4–34 and win the Man-of-the-Match award against Zimbabwe in Nagpur, another match in which the bowlers buckled down and Mark Waugh continued his amazing run of form. Zimbabwe opener Andrew Waller made an enterprising 67, but there was little lasting support and no reason why Australia should not overhaul a modest 154 to win. Which we did, in just 36 overs, after Mark made an unbeaten 76, an innings which took his aggregate for the competition to an extraordinary 332, at an average of 166. He and Mark Taylor reached 50 within 10 overs, and after a 92-run opening stand, there was no logical way Australia could lose.

So far so good, but the next match, against the West Indies in Jaipur, shaped as a really awkward tough proposition. The Windies dearly needed a win if they were going to get past the qualifying stages and already there was widespread gossip of major disagreements in their dressing room. That can work both ways; it can splinter a side or it can bring them together for the hours that they play a match important to their future. With a team as talented and yet as potentially volatile as the Windies, you'd never know. However, they were clearly under a lot of strain.

Jaipur is a remarkable city with distinctly mixed memories for recent Australian visitors. When we played a one-day international there in 1986, Geoff Marsh and David Boon put on a world record 212 for the first wicket — and then India thumped us by seven wickets! That wicket must have been the flattest batting track in India, but this time the pitch was very ordinary; it looked superb but did not play that way. Instead it seamed around and kept low. The outfield was still damp when we batted first, so a total of 229 — thanks chiefly to a splendid 102 from Ricky Ponting — could have been a winning score. In fact, I thought we had enough to win, but the bowlers didn't do their stuff and we managed to lose, as Brian Lara made 60 off 70 deliveries and their captain, Richie Richardson, played fantastically well for 93 not out.

This result ensured the Windies of a place in the quarter-finals, after some critics had written them off. More than that, it was a memorable tribute to Richie Richardson's character. His own form had been poor until then, he had to front up after a chastening defeat by Kenya — for which he publicly apologised to the Caribbean public — and it was common knowledge that there was a lot of infighting in his dressing room. To play as well as he did against a backdrop of disappointment, dissent and some intrigue was a powerful achievement. His contribution became even more significant when he later announced his decision to retire from international cricket at the end of the World Cup. It must have been on his mind when he picked the West Indies up and carried them into the quarter-final stages. Richie was always a respected opponent; the way he carried himself through a desperately difficult World Cup tournament and the dignified way in which he announced his retirement confirmed our admiration for him as a man as well as an international player.

An aside to our match in Jaipur, where our defeat wasn't going to cost us a place in the quarter-finals, was an opportunity to meet up with one of the world's most fascinating women. The mother of the present Maharaja of Jaipur was a world celebrity, wife of the jet-setting Maharaja Man Singh and a woman often described as India's Jacqueline Kennedy. The couple were leading international socialites, in an age of extraordinary wealth, of gold and jewels and swimming pools filled with champagne. On her marriage to Man Singh, she went to live in the Rambagh Palace in Jaipur, still a magnificent building which like so many of the former princely palaces in India has been turned into a luxurious hotel. Her husband, one of the dashing figures of his age, died at a polo match in England and the Maharani was later imprisoned for nearly six months, ostensibly for currency irregularities, but more probably because she was an outspoken political opponent of then Prime Minister, Mrs Indira Gandhi.

The Maharani must be well into her 70s now, but she is still an imposing woman who lives in what was once the pavilion for the tennis courts at the Palace. She has a wonderful store of stories to tell and it is still obvious why she was once described as one of the most beautiful women in the world.

Meanwhile, the practicalities of the tournament were bearing down pretty hard. We had expected security to be tight, having experienced it before, but here it was very strict and sometimes almost stifling. The players were virtually confined to their hotels, which might not matter too much as a rule, but which led to a feeling of being cooped up which was unpleasant and probably unnecessary. The thought of being surrounded by a security wall and being virtually locked in begins to grate.

When we shared a hotel with the Windies players we were guarded by around 150 soldiers and security men! There were at least 25 guards between my room and the hotel foyer and it really wasn't far. Past the guards, through the metal detectors; we wouldn't have been surprised to encounter a couple of minefields. We accepted that these measures were intended for our safety but it would have been easier to take if we had felt threatened in the first place. Our reception wherever we went was warm and very friendly and that made wall-to-wall security seem a bit incongruous. But at the same time, the local newspapers were carrying regular stories about the strife in Sri Lanka — explosions and heightened security measures seemed the order of the day there — so we had to keep the situation in perspective. And we certainly had no cause to regret our decision not to go there.

The Sri Lanka subject seemed to have been dropped by now, although the odd dignitary would suggest we should have gone. I usually asked when India and Pakistan were going to resume normal cricket relations and there was a sudden silence. Screaming headlines about bombs exploding in ambulances and arms dumps found in Colombo didn't exactly suggest we had made a wrong decision.

One thought which did occur most forcibly was that we seemed to be spending more time in transit and overnighting than we did playing cricket. An exaggeration? Probably, but it certainly seemed that way and most countries had a horror story to tell. Take Zimbabwe, who had already copped a disappointing hotel change for the opening ceremony in Calcutta: they went to

Colombo and then took three days to get from there to Patna, which is probably about six hours direct flying time. An overnight in Madras, another in Delhi, it appeared the problem was that Indian Airlines' existing schedules did not dovetail with the tournament program, so teams were sent zigzagging to their next destination. It is hard to believe that smoother arrangements could not have been made, especially bearing in mind that the 1987 Cup went off without a hitch.

After the qualifying rounds we knew we were going to play in Madras, but, only hours before we were due to move, we did not know exactly what our travel itinerary was. So we used a bit of initiative again and ended up in Delhi, which would have been an overnight in any case. As we had a spare couple of days, we organised a trip from Delhi down to Agra and the Taj Mahal — and immediately copped a reprimand from PILCOM for placing the team in danger by ignoring security arrangements. This was odd when you consider that every time we went through Delhi there was no security at all, and we had organised our own security for the Taj trip so that was no problem.

PILCOM also said we had imperilled the tournament transport arrangements and perhaps we had. But if they had told us what the transport arrangements were, it would have been easier to stick to them. New Zealand, our opponents in Madras, had arrived in Delhi 12 hours after us, when it seemed they could have been put on the same plane. And, after they lost their quarter-final, the Kiwis found that no immediate travel arrangements were in place, so they had to spend nearly a week kicking their heels before heading off to London en route to their tour of the Caribbean. They were furious and rightly so.

The way the competition draw had been structured it was obvious right from the start who the quarter-final teams were going to be. That is not necessarily unfair, as there is a strong element of seeding in many international tournaments, and it clearly makes good financial sense. However, perhaps because of the inevitability of the draw, there had been precious few really exciting matches in the qualifying rounds. The obvious exception, of course, was Kenya's win over the West Indies — and the thrills that game generated came because of the result rather than the cricket.

One-day cricket craves close finishes, and because so many matches were one-sided the general feeling was that the competition was a little disappointing. The chief culprit was probably the pitches: they were prepared to help batsmen, not surprisingly, but they were generally overdone and too flat. Early batsmen got off to raging starts, in fact I doubt there had ever been a

World Cup in which so many top-order batsmen scored so many runs so quickly. And that naturally led to a superficial view that the best tactic was big hitters at the start of the innings, with batsmen swinging from ball one. Yet, nobody was more explosive than Mark Waugh. The quality of his performances, and the way he played, only added weight to our belief that a skilful batsman playing enterprisingly will beat a hopeful slogger any day of the week. Mark was positive and dynamic, nobody more so, but he did not alter his style significantly from the way he normally plays.

The pitches were so good that a player of his calibre in his form was going to take a dreadful toll of anything but the very best bowling. It has to be said that a lot of the bowling in the 1996 World Cup was sub-standard. No disrespect to any batsman who did well, but the general bowling standard fell well below previous tournaments; there seemed to be a lack of accuracy and a lack of imagination.

The quarter-finals lifted the tempo of the tournament considerably, if only because sudden-death situations instil their own drama and the crowds began to identify with their own teams and the favourites they had established among the rival countries. Naturally, some matches were better than others and we had the opportunity to watch them because the scheduling gave us free time and we were able to install ourselves in front of television sets.

The previously unbeaten South Africans were competition favourites when they met the West Indies in Karachi, but when it came to the death they looked a bit complacent. That, at least, was the impression I got from the box, from the body language of the players. West Indies made 264 on the back of a century from Brian Lara, not a huge total and one which looked well within South Africa's reach. But then they lost four wickets in two overs, and slid from an apparently-commanding 4–196 to a position where they needed 22 runs from the last over. Mission impossible, of course, but I'm still not entirely sure how they managed to squander a winning position. That's one-day cricket for you. Hansie Cronje said later that he would willingly swap any of their previous victories for a quarter-final win, and it does seem particularly tough when your first defeat puts you out of the Cup.

England went out to Sri Lanka, thrashed by five wickets with nearly 10 overs to spare in Faisalabad. The Sri Lankans' Sanath Jayasuriya did the damage with an extraordinary 82 from only 44 balls, but throughout the competition it was clear that England had lost the plot. They simply did not seem to have a concerted approach or a game plan they were prepared to stick to all the way through; they seemed to be looking for some magic formula rather than backing themselves as English pros once would. The old English professional in trouble used to go back to basics and fight his way out; England at this World Cup lacked direction and any recognisable policy. There must have been a whole load of theories wafting round the dressing room, because the cricket they played did not have a recognisable theme or a clear common-sense factor.

Watching from a distance, it seemed to me that they lacked what hard-nosed Yorkshiremen used to call 'nous'. This is particularly odd when you consider the selection chairman and team manager was Ray Illingworth, pretty well the public image of what a Yorkshire cricketer is supposed to be. It was never clear, however, just who was leading whom; they seemed to stagger from match to match looking desperately for some magic ingredient which would relieve them of the responsibility of having to play well. Against Sri Lanka, England promoted all-rounder Phil de Freitas ahead of Alec Stewart and Jack Russell in the batting order and he responded with an invaluable 67 to help lift them to 235. Fair enough in the circumstances, but it showed how unsettled England's batting line-up had become; blokes who might normally be good for 20s were being asked to go up the order and do the batsmen's job.

England's situation wasn't made any easier by the fact that two of their best batsmen, captain Mike Atherton and Alec Stewart, had poor tournaments, a surprise when you consider that they are both consistent players who don't normally play too many false shots. They're good strikers of the ball, too. Atherton, in particular, looked very vulnerable and in the quarter-final played a whole series of shots well outside his normal range. He looked to me like a man unsure of how he should be playing, and it's a bit late to explore that when you are out in the middle. Even on flat pitches he seemed capable of getting a nick on deliveries which nearly qualified as wides, all the more surprising since he had come off a very good Test series against South Africa. The fact that he and Stewart did not fire put a lot of pressure on the batting order and it was clear that England never developed a strategy to compensate. This was England's worst World Cup performance; even when they won, I cannot remember them looking convincing.

India versus Pakistan was always going to be a huge drawcard and their quarter-final at Bangalore attracted its share of publicity off the field. Both sides were making suitably conciliatory noises and the fans were deterred by a baton-charge from storming the gates after the 'house full' signs went up. No doubt the organisers would have loved an India-Pakistan final, but the way the draw fell in the later stages there was no chance of that. It was a tight match with plenty of feeling on the pitch — you could register the body language even if the words didn't mean anything — and some of our players wondered what officialdom's reaction would have been if any other team had been involved. Much stricter, for sure.

India made 287, based on 93 from their opener, Navjot Sidhu, and a flailing 45 from Ajay Jadeja in mid-order. Pakistan conceded 62 runs off their last five overs, which was significant because the match was there to be won by the mentally tougher side. India's bowlers took some punishment, but kept their heads; they were temperamentally stronger on the day and eventually won by 39 runs.

The Chepauk/Chidambaram stadium in Madras has assumed a special place in Australia's cricket history over the last decade. It was an experience in 1996 to be going back there for Madras' first day-night international match, at the ground where we scored an amazing victory two World Cups ago and where we played an even more amazing tied Test in 1986. The place has changed a bit, but it still looked eerily familiar. And it smells better these days! My abiding non-cricket memory of the ground will always be the pervading stench that was provided by the nearby Buckingham Canal, an open waterway which was little more than a sewer and certainly gave the stadium a distinctive air. The canal has now disappeared, silted up over the years and now filled in and redeveloped as the route of a railway line that runs through the centre of the city.

We were confident of beating New Zealand, but we knew they had nothing to lose. And they certainly came out with all guns blazing, in what developed into a gripping match which really set the tournament alight. They were without bowlers Danny Morrison and Gavin Larsen and obviously knew they needed a very big score to give them a chance. We had them 3–44 and in serious trouble, but Chris Harris played the innings of his life and the captain, Lee Germon, pushed himself up the order and really took it up to the bowlers. Harris scored 130 from 130 deliveries, quite extraordinary considering he had totalled just 26 runs in the World Cup so far, while Germon made 89 from 91. Their partnership of 168 was the highest for the fourth wicket in the World Cup and, partiality aside, I thought it was a performance of tremendous character and determination. Some of their shot-making was superb and it was just as well, not that we doubted it, that we had a ready reply in Mark Waugh.

Mark's third century in five Cup matches wasn't really a surprise; he was in such good form and frame of mind that on a good batting strip like this nobody was going to stop him unless he made a silly mistake. He made 110 off 112 deliveries, became the first batsman to score three centuries in one World Cup competition on the way, and never gave the New Zealand attack a look-in. This was another innings to be added to Australia's role of honour in Madras.

Two days later, Calcutta became a nightmare for cricket in India — for the organisers who could not control a semi-final crowd despite the saturation presence of police and paramilitary security forces and for an Indian captain who made the most amazing tactical decision of the World Cup competition. By the time the match had degenerated into a dangerous farce, rightly awarded to Sri Lanka in defiance of mob rule, Mohammad Azharuddin's decision to bowl after winning the toss probably seemed irrelevant. However, if India had been in a position to win the match the riots would never have happened. Irrelevant? Hardly.

For the best part of a month, the square at Eden Gardens had been under the stage laid for the World Cup opening ceremony. Everybody knew it and it was common talk among the teams that the pitch would be anybody's guess for the semi-final. Nobody really knew how it would react and, certainly, it looked pretty good on the surface. But expert opinion — and local knowledge was as available to 'Azhar' as to anybody else — was that it would become more difficult as the match progressed. Win the toss and bat. No question.

If Azhar was given any advice he must have ignored it and, having put Sri Lanka in, he was blitzed by a whirlwind 66 off only 47 deliveries by Sri Lanka's Aravinda de Silva. Sri Lanka had not begun in their usual raging way, not with both openers out in the first over, but their middle-order played like men who knew conditions could only get worse. Despite their appalling start, the pitch had played easily for the visitors and with a total of 251, they sensed they were in the box seat.

India were 8–120 in 34 overs and about to lose the match badly on what had become a difficult turning pitch when the crowd erupted. As wicket followed wicket, the crowd which had cheered India's every move in the field became dismayed and sullen. The flag-waving and boisterousness gave way to frustration and anger. Fires were lit in the stands, then bottles sailed over the fence.

The match referee was former West Indian captain Clive Lloyd, who has seen enough ugly crowds in his time to recognise the danger in the situation, which was not coming from a majority of spectators but certainly from some hotheads who were already threatening the Sri Lankan fieldsmen near the boundary. Near the end, Ranatunga moved Aravinda de Silva away from the fence and put the 12th man Chandra Uppal there instead — obviously 12th men are expendable

— and the substitute was lucky when a bottle sailed just past him. Lloyd really had no option but to take the players off the field and once he had done that, there was precious little chance of any sort of a resumption. The safety of the players had to be his first consideration and, obviously, that could not be guaranteed. Sri Lanka were poised to win in any case so the match clearly had to be awarded to them. And the point had to be made that spectators cannot take matters into their own hands and stop a match if their side is losing, in the hope that it might be abandoned or replayed.

We watched the match on television from our hotel in Chandigarh and did not get a full picture of just how bad the atmosphere was or how serious was the threat to the Sri Lankan players. Cricket is at the mercy of a minority who want to cause trouble; the most stringent security precautions will not prevent trouble if the crowd decides to look for it. That has been proven time and time again and Eden Gardens that night was an obvious example of the limitations of so-called 'blanket' security. The place was crawling with security forces and the ground is ringed by a high fence, yet the players on the pitch were still vulnerable.

It is not uncommon in India and Pakistan for streets to be cordoned off well away from the ground, for individual searches of those going to the game, for metal detectors to be employed. However, you cannot confiscate every coin or every box of matches and the masses of people involved means that a resourceful villain will get through.

This was a thought which occurred quite naturally to a group of players who had been branded as cowards for refusing to accept reassurances of total security in Colombo. The events in Calcutta that night, sad and deplorable as they were, exposed the realities of trying to police a big and volatile crowd on the sub-continent. Can anyone seriously believe that the security guards in Sri Lanka would have been able to stop a determined and trained terrorist in an area where terrorism has become a fact of everyday life? Calcutta is regarded as one of the safer grounds in India, as far as security and the sporting attitudes of the local crowd are concerned, yet the match had to be abandoned. And it could have been much worse.

The ground at Mohali outside Chandigarh is the newest and probably the best in India. Facilities are splendid, a great deal of sensible planning has obviously gone into developing the arena and the practice conditions were first class, almost as good as those at the Adelaide Oval, which is a rare compliment.

The only question mark before our semi-final against the West Indies involved the floodlights. The ground is practically next door to an air force base, so it is hardly appropriate to erect half a dozen 20-metre towers on the flight path. Instead, the ground was ringed by 18 banks of lights, each around 12 metres high. Whatever the watts, lux and candlepower theories involved, the fact is that players on both sides struck a problem with glare with the ball in the air. I am not sure what can be done about that but more international matches are sure to be played at the ground and if a vital catch goes down because of the low lights there will be a row for sure. In the semi-final, the Windies' Shivnarine Chanderpaul seemed to lose one lofted drive when Stuart Law and Michael Bevan were going so well for Australia; it might have been important.

Some experts installed the West Indies as favourites before the match, partly because they had come on strongly after their chastening defeat by Kenya and partly because it was argued that Australia must be tired after our tough quarter-final, which had come at the end of almost seven months continuous cricket. Well, we expected a tough Cup tournament and we prepared ourselves that way, so we were not about to make excuses about being tired. And when one scribe wrote that, 'no strategy, no amount of training and no manner of motivation can stand the test of the West Indies' brilliance,' we certainly were not prepared to go along with that.

It was a phenomenal game of cricket. We were gone, but staged a great fightback and made just enough runs to give ourselves something to bowl at. Then the West Indies seemed set to stroll to victory. And Australia pulled off a miraculous win. Five runs! That's all Australia had to play with when the Windies' last man, Courtney Walsh, was bowled by Damien Fleming. It was as complete a defence of a vulnerable score as you could wish to see, a thoroughly professional performance, especially, I thought, by Glenn McGrath.

Nobody would argue with Shane Warne's right to be named Man of the Match, after he picked up 4–36 and swung the match around with three wickets in three vital overs near the end. McGrath, though, bowled tightly and applied a lot of pressure, which was particularly pleasing because he had endured a very ordinary time in the tournament up to then. Glenn convinced himself that he was going to run in hard and bowl naturally and was a very important factor in the win.

Paul Reiffel and Fleming also did a big job, in a situation where nobody could afford to bowl a really bad ball, while our fielding returned to that level of attitude and excellence which had set world standards. The pitch was a bit lively, which was a huge help when we bowled because it meant the fielding side was always in with a bit of a chance. The West Indies had bowled well on it and we would have been steamrollered out of the semi-final except for a tremendous partnership between Law and Bevan, who picked us up from disaster at 4–15 and put on 138 invaluable runs. Stuart made 72 off 105 deliveries and Michael 69 off 109 and without them this would not have been a match. As it was, our total of 207 did not exactly look impregnable.

It would be pushing the truth a bit — a fair bit — to say that I always expected us to win. However, I sensed long before the end of the West Indies innings that they were beginning to crack. It had looked as though they had to win when Lara and Chanderpaul hoisted them to 2–165, but Australia were giving nothing away in the field and the attitude of every player remained fierce and aggressive. Nobody looked as though he expected to lose. Whenever a West Indian batsman contemplated a run he took a risk; whenever he eyeballed an Australian he found himself looking at a bloke who stared back defiantly and radiated strength and determination. The Australians had a sniff of victory and the Windies knew it; the batsmen's body language became nervous and anxious. Some of our fieldsmen looked as though they would arrive before the ball.

The cracks appeared and widened, and their innings collapsed in an amazing cloud of debris, as eight wickets fell for 37 runs in 8.2 overs, with pandemonium breaking loose in the crowd and both dressing rooms in a state of torture. The West Indies needed only six runs to win off five balls when Curtly Ambrose launched himself for a run and Ian Healy's underarmed throw broke the stumps. The third umpire deliberated and then the red light flashed on. Out! Talk about tension. Ian admitted afterwards several players on the field thought Ambrose was safe.

One delivery later it was all over — the best match of the 1996 World Cup and the one which will be remembered not only by Australian supporters, but by anyone who saw it, either live or on television — and we are talking about something approaching half a billion people, easily the biggest television audience ever for a game of cricket. Afterwards, it seemed that everyone we met had seen the dramatic finale on television and, although too many of India's 900 million population are obscenely poor, it is worth remembering that over 300 million have what the advertising men call 'disposable income' and some are very rich indeed. This is what excites the sponsors: the thought of 50 million TV sets and, I understand, over 18 million cable TV sets… that, in anybody's currency, is a goldmine.

To the final in Lahore, where Sri Lanka were too good for us. Simple as that. Of course, it was a huge disappointment after the exceptional efforts the boys had put into their Cup campaign, but I do not subscribe to any theories about the team being wearied by their build-up to the final. They had performed brilliantly to get out of jail on more than one occasion and, no doubt, those efforts took something out of them which was hard to replace or repeat when it mattered most. But being able to do that is what winning international cricket competitions is all about.

There was a great deal in Australia's performances through the World Cup to convince me that at our best we are the best team in the world, but nobody wins every match and there is no need to excuse a flat performance as other than what it was. Perhaps more than that, it might have been a complacent one. After a couple of miraculous wins, there may have been a feeling that it was Australia's fate to win the Cup, that whatever the players were touching it would automatically turn to gold. We talked about complacency, of course, warned against it, swore it could never happen. However, I had an uneasy feeling that it was implanted in some minds.

In a perverse way, the fact that Mark Taylor got Australia's innings off to such a galloping start might have strengthened the belief that this was a match we were going to win, come what may. No criticism of Mark in that, of course, who attacked from the start and finished with 74. He led from the front and with the innings racing along at somewhere around six an over, it looked as though a total of at least 280, perhaps 300, was on the cards. Mark and Ricky Ponting put on 101 from just 115 deliveries, which was almost outrageous, but the innings lost its way and nobody seemed capable of reviving our early momentum. We fell into the bad habit of hitting too many shots too firmly to fieldsmen and let the Sri Lankans bowl at us, which contrasted with the way we had been pushing the ball around brilliantly in previous matches.

The Sri Lankan spinners delivered the ball tightly and it took us far too long to re-establish a common-sense approach. We needed to go back to the basics, find the gaps, manufacture a-run-a-ball, but we wasted a lot of time reaffirming this principle. It was decided to send in Shane Warne at number five, as a pinch-hitter, but I thought this was unnecessary. Ninety-nine times out of a hundred I think it's pointless to promote a hitter to do what a batsman should do better, and I've said that often enough. Some people swear by this tactic and regard it as a sign of inventive thinking, but experience has warned me against it. I have seldom seen the hit men succeed. If the decision is taken and it works I would put my hand up and say: 'You were right, I was wrong. It came off this time and well done.' But I really don't think I'd need to say that too often. On balance I'd vote against the pinch-hitter and Mark Taylor knows my feelings well enough.

It is a move, though, that the captain must make himself, for he is the one who is going to cop the kudos or the kicks up the backside. Mark made the decision and there was no conflict. It could even have been a decision backed by most of the players. My view was that we were going okay, a couple of wickets notwithstanding, and a more qualified batsman was more equipped to consolidate our position and push the score along. As it turned out, Shane was quickly dismissed. I believe a wicket, even if it is number nine batting at number five, gives the bowling side a lift. But decisions have to be taken in the heat of battle. Mark did what he thought was right and the captain has to do that. When it comes to pinch-hitters, we will probably agree to differ…

As usual, there was plenty unusual about the final. The night before there was a formidable storm and there was considerable doubt about whether the match would be able to start on time. There was also a query over the ability of the local electricity board to supply power to the floodlights for the whole of the final. It should be okay, they said, but there were no guarantees and we feared the worst when the lights were dimmed for a while. They insisted they were simply giving the lights a rest and who were we to argue. However, it didn't look as though the lights would last the distance. There was an awful lot of 'to-ing and fro-ing' during the match, even in the posh restricted seats, and loud arguments broke out from time to time while well-heeled ticketholders argued their right to occupy the seats they thought they had paid for. Nepotism is alive and well in Pakistan cricket and a few celebrities found their seats already occupied by people holding special passes from all sorts of influential officials. Nobody who has toured Pakistan finds that unusual and the local newspapers love to run little asides in their columns listing the fat cats who were embarrassed by the arrangements.

Mark Taylor and I had been down to the ground early, fearing the worst after heavy overnight rain, and we were frankly amazed to find the ground in good enough condition for the match to start at the scheduled time. We whistled up the team from the hotel and they hustled down to the Gaddafi stadium in good time.

The overnight downpour did not help the fieldsmen, but not immediately, so this fact worked to the advantage of the team which fielded first. This was because, when the lights came on, they drew moisture from below. So, if you ran your palms over the ground and they became slick, and the ball became slippery. However, even allowing for this occurrence, we could have won if we had taken our catches. A couple went down which would normally have been taken which is what responding to pressure is all about. It is not an excuse. We would beat Sri Lanka seven times out of 10, but on the day that mattered they were better than us; there's no getting away from it.

A great deal was made of the Sri Lankans' aggressive attitude right from the first ball, but there was more depth to their game than that. They lost 2–23 in the final and still beat us by seven wickets with all of 3.4 overs to spare, which indicates how sensibly Asanka Gurusinha, Ranatunga and especially de Silva approached their task. De Silva is a magnificent batsman when he has his mind focused. He had involved himself in too much confrontation during Sri Lanka's tour of Australia, which badly affected his batting, but with his mind on cricket he really did have a wonderful World Cup; his batting in the last two innings was as skilful and accomplished as any player in the game.

Overall, we were disappointed with our performances because we did not hit our real standard often enough during the Cup and we certainly didn't sustain it. The team grabbed some famous victories and showed real character in the way they sometimes got out of jail, but we did not always play to our potential. The fielding was okay, but not consistently up to the standards we have developed over the years. No excuses, though, not even the easy one that all the political wrangling disturbed our focus before the competition; we could have done without it but I don't think it affected the players once the decisions were made and we got down to work. And, given the circumstances at the time, I'm sure the decisions that were made were the right ones.

The consensus of opinion after the tournament was that the event in Pakistan was better organised than in India and that the organisation overall was not a patch on 1987. Of course, anyone who discusses such facts is liable to be accused of whingeing, but I heard very little of that from the players. Certainly, the Australian boys were magnificent in the way they accepted the niggles and nuisances and got on with their job. The organising committee, PILCOM, made too many mistakes but they did also made a huge amount of money. And without doubt, that will be a lever used to encourage the ICC to stage more international tournaments in the sub-continent.

The figures being bandied about after the Cup were amazing. Nobody doubted that money played a big part in the decision where to hold the tournament in the first place and the profits said to be generated were quite mind-boggling. The Indian Cricket Board, so rich but based in a country scarred by poverty, stood to profit to the tune of $US100 million. A Connecticut-based sports management firm, World Tel, had bid $US10 million for the TV rights and resold them internationally for $US23 million. The tournament's major sponsor, Wills, forked out the equivalent of nearly $US12 million for naming rights to the World Cup. Coca Cola, named as the 'official soft drink' of the Cup, paid $US3.7 million for the privilege of exclusive pouring rights inside the stadia. Visa paid $US350,000 to be named as an official supplier. The list went on and on. So the World Cup generated a huge amount of money and if money talks — which is where we came in — the case for playing important tournaments in the sub-continent is obvious. But huge profits do not justify substandard organisation or risks to visiting teams. Money should not be the only consideration.

I still have a copy of an article which appeared in a newspaper in India during the World Cup. Im my opinion, it could have been usefully published in every cricket-playing country of the world. It was not written by a jaundiced visitor to the country, or by a player paid for a newspaper column and anxious to plead his own case for a bigger share of World Cup riches. It was written by R. Mohan, India's leading cricket journalist and a man who obviously shares the belief that revenue is not an end in itself. It is worth reproducing in full…

The only good thing about the worst Press box in the Wills World Cup is the view. The one reason why Lee Germon may have wished to go to the middle quickly was that he did not have, to begin with, as good a view of the game. Maybe that is why he stayed on so long to make his highest one-day score.

Having won the toss and seized the chance to bat, the Kiwi captain was busy looking for a chair and some view of the game. He could not get to see the whole playing area of the Chepauk ground from the area earmarked for his team. He found the passage at the far end of the pavilion was one spot from which he could actually see the game.

Soon, the Kiwis gathered there to make their own player box. But what else could they do if they wished to see the match in which they were, incidentally, playing. Surely, the captain and the batsmen going in to bat would like to sit at some vantage point from where they can watch the proceedings. All this must have seemed curious for the cricketers of a nation to whose amenities a lot of attention is paid although their board, New Zealand Cricket, is not exactly swelling in the coffers. Far from it.

The lack of concern for player amenities, and not to forget media facilities, is further testimony to which direction cricket is going now in this country. It is the commerce which puts money in the game but it is the greed of administrators which is responsible for such shabby treatment of an international team.

The game is greater than the players but would there be a game at all if there are no players. What has been lost sight of as the sub continental World Cup draws to a close is the raison d'etre of cricket. The players make the game and the people come to watch them at cricket.

What happens when the administration decides to make a fast buck is such basic facilities as an unhindered view of the game are denied even to players. It is nice to know that the ticket sales have been to the tune of (over 10 million rupees) for a match between Australia and New Zealand in Madras which goes to show how sports minded the people are. But is money everything?

It is not in basic facilities alone that the best players of 12 nations in the World Cup are being denied. They are being short-changed in the matter of payments for participation in the competition… The megabucks being spoken of in this event are obviously for the organisation of the competition and for the boards but not for the players who are the ones the people are coming out to watch in such numbers.

The television explosion has done much for cricket in terms of rights revenues… The ten-fold expansion of revenue on this account alone is not reflected in the prize money… Clive Lloyd used to say that all his team got for winning the first two Prudential (World) Cups was a cup and not much more. His team was not fortunate to the extent Kapil Dev's men were when they got a little more from the largesse of the public and the supporters of the game (for winning the Cup in 1983) than from the cricket board of the time which showered the team with tributes more than financial reward. Much that was promised by State governments by way of land allotment did not come through at all.

The Australians led by Allan Border benefited little in terms of money by winning the Reliance (World) Cup though the victory did a lot for them by way of lifting their cricket prestige and the consequent rise of public interest in the team's fortunes which has led to the players getting a better deal now.

Mark Taylor's men get fair financial terms in their contract with the board. Still, it is only the stars who sweep away the endorsement money which alone makes the game worthwhile for the likes of Shane Warne, Brian Lara and Sachin Tendulkar. They are in a different league altogether. They talk about millions in a year.

The boards have little to do with their star value which the public fixes and which commerce boosts by way of endorsements from manufacturers of just about everything — from soft drinks through sporting apparel to training shoes and even shoe polish.

The burgeoning middle class of India which laps up white goods makes such endorsement deals even more lucrative for Tendulkar, who now commands as much as half a million dollars for sporting a logo on his bat which he will be doing shortly and soon after the World Cup during which he does not want anything to upset his focus.

Australia's cricket coach Bob Simpson who was some sort of a common factor in two ties Tests in the first of which he was a player and in the second the team's cricket manager, is flabbergasted by the figures of Tendulkar's cricket earnings. But even such figures pale in comparison to what stars earn in tennis, golf, boxing, baseball and basketball.

The point is that while commerce has brought in so much to the World Cup and endorsements to the stars, very little will trickle down to the many others who go out there and play the game so well as to attract spectators in their thousands and a television audience in hundreds of millions. While that itself is a pity, why deny them even the basics as the Tamil Nadu Cricket Association did in its hunt for profit in millions.

While almost every other association has gone out of the way to improve player and media facilities it appears an association with such a great tradition of players and game orientation has lost its way. Grace is conspicuous by its absence. A pity, because it was not always like this. There used to be a certain pride in organising cricket at Chepauk. Now Mammon rules. So they count the space available in terms of square feet and squeeze out even the players' view while squeezing in more people and, obviously, squeezing out more money.

CHAPTER 12

Despite what you may have read in sections of the media, Bob Simpson was not booted out of the job as Australian coach kicking and screaming and desperately pulling strings to try and cling on. I wanted to continue in the job because I thought it was a particularly bad time to change direction; I made that clear then and I make no bones about it now. But I wish Geoff Marsh and the team every success and I wish some of my critics would concern themselves with the facts and not with personal prejudice.

So these critics don't like Simmo. So what? My job was to help restore Australian cricket, not to win popularity contests. When I was accused of being a politician, it was usually by people I had confronted and told publicly they had got something wrong. Some politician! I am not immune from criticism and neither is anyone in the media — but I take exception when opinions are reported as facts, when I am misquoted and when facts are trimmed to suit a reporter's campaigning views. How professional are the people who do that?

Ian Chappell has been my rent-a-quote critic for many years. He is entitled to his views. I got on well with Ian when I captained him in the Australian side, always found him ready to express his views and take advice, and I acted as a sort of agent for the Australian teams he captained after my first 'retirement'. Ian was ambitious, he wanted to be Australia's captain — nothing wrong with that — and we had more than one long chat about what he should do to achieve it.

Unfortunately, our relationship changed after the World Series Cricket split; some of the stars who joined WSC resented the negative reaction their decision caused in many areas, and they still bear grudges. Ian has spouted for ages that Test-quality players do not need coaching but that did not prevent him taking up a coaching — sorry, consultant — position with Pakistan. Greg Chappell coached (or perhaps consulted) with the Australian A team and then said the job of Test coach was redundant — but, he added, he just might be interested in an associated role if it came up.

Both Chappells retain a high profile in Australian cricket, and have the opportunity to push their barrow through their roles as commentators on Channel Nine. I wonder, though, what they really left behind for the game's next generation when their playing careers ended. A generation of players with obvious ability and potential — cricketers such as Graham Yallop, Ian Davis, Peter Toohey and even Kim Hughes — were the young residual from the Chappells' era who never really fulfilled their promise. Greg, a wonderful player, was unable to lead Queensland to the Sheffield Shield although they had the best team at the time. Perhaps this was because he was not a great communicator of skills.

When I became Australia's coach, I looked around for people who could improve the quality of the team's performance. Because Ian had publicly stated on many occasions that he does not believe in coaching at the elite level, we never formally asked him to contribute. However, others of that era did have an input — Dennis Lillee, for instance, had an open invitation to help out and he made a big contribution. Brendon Julian, for one, benefited enormously from Lillee's help on the 1993 Ashes tour. So some players help, some contribute beyond their playing days and some just sit in judgment. I know which is the easiest option.

Australian Cricket is about to enter one of its most difficult periods and I fear that Geoff Marsh has been handed a very demanding job two years before he is ready for it. Geoff will be a fine coach one day, I have absolutely no doubts about that. He has the background and all the personal qualities the job needs, assuming that he is going to be rather more than just a helper and a sidekick for the captain. But the fact is that Geoff has no coaching experience to fall back on — and the next few years will be very difficult and perhaps a little chastening for some members of the squad.

The present Australian team, good as it is, cannot go on for much longer. Several players are nearing the end of their careers and will come under a lot of pressure from the young bloods. At the same time, the program is fiendishly busy — between August 1996 and April 1998 the team will be playing just about all the time — and the atmosphere round the team will be pretty hectic. Very challenging, of course, but also fraught with dangers. Players nearing the end of their career know that they are under pressure and, human nature being what it is, they react in different and sometimes blinkered ways. The transition to a new-look Australian team — encouraging talented youngsters without wasting any of the experience the stalwarts can offer — will not be easy.

That was why I urged the ACB to give me another two years as coach. I felt the team needed continuity and solidarity at this particular time. My suggestion was that I continue as coach with Geoff as assistant until after the 1997 Ashes tour, when I would step aside if everything was working okay. That would help ease Geoff into the job, allow me to show him the ropes and bring him closer to the off-field paraphernalia of international cricket. Believe me, that is quite a revelation when you have seen the game only from a player's perspective. It seemed like common sense to me, although it was misrepresented in some quarters as an attempt by me to cling on regardless.

I read in the media that I tried to 'lobby' the Board to renew my role, how I used all kinds of political machinations to try and get my own way. In fact, I was asked how I saw the future and spelled it out in a letter to the Board shortly before I left, soon after the 1996 World Cup, for an overseas holiday. Most certainly, I wanted to keep the job. I made no secret of that and I outlined my reasons as carefully as I could in a five-page letter to the Board. Why not? They were about to make a decision on my future and I would be away on holiday when the relevant Board meeting was held. As it turned out, the timing of the holiday was unfortunate — hence the letter — but it was the only chance I would have to take a break if my contract was renewed. The notion that I was hawking myself around, cap in hand, was utter rubbish. Whenever my contract as coach had been due for renewal over the years, it had always been a matter of discussion and exchange of ideas with the members of the Board. There were never any formal written applications. This was what happened in 1996 as well. In my 43 years in first-class Australian cricket, I never once applied for a job.

In January 1996, I suggested to Graham Halbish, the ACB's chief executive, that we should sort out my position before we left for the World Cup. I preferred to know where I stood, as I knew there would be speculation in the media which might not help us through the tournament. I had heard that my contract would be discussed after the World Cup, which would end in mid-March, and this was confirmed by Graham (and accepted, reluctantly, by me). So, when we returned from the sub-continent, I met him and the Board chairman, Denis Rogers, in Melbourne.

It was at this point that I became aware that they had already mapped out an alternative role for me. It seemed they had decided that the new Australian coach would be less of a 'guru' — as they put it — and more of an assistant to the captain. After all the time and money the Board had spent developing a sound coaching system, such a move seemed illogical to say the least. And the timing was particularly bad, given Australia's imposing international program. I put my thoughts in a letter dated April 19th, and sent it to Halbish, asking him to circulate it to all Board members. The letter was handed to the members when they sat down for the Board meeting, almost a month later, on May 15th.

The only real reason I was given for the decision taken that day was that it was 'time for a change'. This seems pretty shallow reasoning to me. Take this to its logical conclusion and there will come a time when Board members and even chief executives are sacked because it is time for a change. Or leg-spin bowlers. Perhaps even journalists and TV commentators who have been around for 10 years will automatically get the boot. So what price experience? I still don't accept this point, but apart from some general remarks about my health it was all I was offered by way of explanation. The offer of another, less 'hands-on' role was attractive and certainly worth a lot of thought, but I had been directly involved in cricket for a lifetime and my enthusiasm for getting out on the field was as strong as ever. I know I will miss it.

IF EVER A BLOKE DESERVED TO SUCCEED IN LIFE, THAT BLOKE IS GEOFF MARSH.

As I sit down to write about 'Swampy' I realise that he will hardly be remembered as a player by future generations weaned on the more glamorous and exciting players in the Australian side. He may be remembered as a fine coach; only time will tell. Whatever he achieves in his new role, it will be a travesty if Geoff does not get the credit he deserves for his enormous influence on Australian cricket at a time when it had to pull itself up by its bootstraps, at a time when the side needed all the character and stability it could get. We sometimes talk about Merv Hughes as the heart of the Australian side of his era. For the best part of a decade, Swampy was the backbone.

Geoff's natural talents were very limited. I don't say that to put him down because he was a wonderful example of what you can achieve without being a genius, so long as you work hard and put 110 per cent into everything you do. A coach would not offer Mark Waugh as a role model for kids because he has a special talent which very few in the game will match. In contrast, Geoff Marsh became a formidable international cricketer by using every ounce of his ability and showing the sort of determination that wins wars. Swampy wanted desperately to be a Test player and he eventually became a very good one. He is an outstanding example of the man whose desire conquered every obstacle. His contemporaries liked him as a bloke and looked up to him as a player because they recognised the character that went into his game. Many of them were far more talented than he was, but none of them would claim to be better. We knew they were, he knew they were, but nobody ever, ever underestimated what he put into the side.

Swampy was the bridge and the buffer between the team and the captain — and that was a crucial role at a time when Allan Border was coming to grips with what he was and wanted to be. When the 'Captain Grumpy' mood descended on AB, Swampy would invariably take the weight and the spotlight off the captain, lighten the atmosphere and focus the team on something that had to be done. He was a very determined character, his own man, and he read AB like a book, which is significant when you consider that he probably never finished another book in his life! This was because he had a streak of nervous energy which prevented him sitting in the same place for long; he could focus on cricket and play long innings under pressure but off the field he had a restlessness about him which sometimes drove others crazy.

It was not unusual for Geoff to ring the physio at 3am for a chat and 'how about a cup of tea?' His perennial room-mate, David Boon, once woke up in the small hours during the 1989 Ashes tour to find Swampy, bollock naked, practising his shots in front of the mirror. Outwardly Swampy always looked calm and serene, but there was a really hard drive inside which compelled him to want to improve, to play every match as though it was his first and last for Australia. He was the perfect vice-captain at a time when being the Australian vice-captain was not easy. He treasured the position and regarded it as a real honour.

As a batsman, Geoff suffered at first from the sheer intensity of his desire to hold down a place in the team and do well. One of the first things we had to work on was his grip on the bat; he did not hold the bat so much as strangle it! You could see the strain in his knotted forearm muscles; sometimes he even complained of cramps. He was prone to get out in the cover-point area, driving with his bottom hand working overtime. But Geoff worked at the problem as hard as he worked at everything else, including his fielding. He was the original iron hands when he first broke into the Australian side, but he spent hours practising his catching and made himself into one of the finest gully fieldsmen in the game.

His persistence spoke volumes for his mental drive and determination, and, quite simply, for his love of the game. Every player, even the most dedicated, has a day when he cannot switch on, when playing cricket for a living becomes a chore. Every player except Geoff Marsh, that is. He was always the first to say 'C'mon, lets get out there and do it.' I cannot recall him ever complaining about the workload or whingeing about pressures, real or imaginary. Like AB, he just loved to get out and play the game. They shared a great zest for cricket, which may be why he read the captain's moods so well.

It is not generally known, but Geoff had the toughest assignment ever offered to a vice-captain on the Ashes tour of 1989 — leading the side against Lancashire at Old Trafford the day after Australia won the first Test of the series. The team had enjoyed some serious celebrations after their win, and next morning were still tired and emotional. With a couple of exceptions, you have never seen a more bedraggled set of bog-eyed cricketers and, with AB having the game off, captain Swampy certainly had a job on his hands. Lancashire won the toss and batted, and very early in the day David Boon set new standards at short leg by dropping the easiest catch of the tour. It ballooned high into the air, but instead of snapping it up, Boonie toppled decorously forward until his helmet fell over his eyes and the ball hit him on the forearm.

Swampy was shaking his head, clapping his hands between overs and telling everybody to get a grip. Then an edge flew straight between his hands and belted him on the chest! I reckon we dropped five catches before lunch, with Swampy all the while desperately trying to keep a straight face and lead from the front. Eventually we won the match by nine wickets, but not before the county's two imported quicks, Wasim Akram of Pakistan and the West Indies' Patrick Patterson were warned off for bowling too many bouncers... at poor old Geoff, of course.

Swampy had a reputation for slow scoring which was not altogether undeserved, but he knew his role in the side and that included getting centuries in Test matches rather than flashy fifties. In the one-day game we worked on the principle that if one of the early batsmen scored a century, even if that innings absorbed quite a few overs, that would form the basis for a formidable team score. Geoff scored nine one-day international centuries, which when he retired was more than any other Australian batsman, and despite his detractors he played some magnificent one-day innings.

None was better than 113 off 140 deliveries against the Windies in Bridgetown in 1991. Swampy hit eight fours and three sixes that day, including a monumental stroke off Malcolm Marshall which cleared the roof of the stand beyond long-on. I recall one reporter asking AB afterwards if he was surprised by Geoff's big hitting and Border looking genuinely surprised at the question. 'Why wouldn't he?' our captain remarked. 'He is a farmer, you know.' Geoff was very strong and hit some of the longest sixes I have seen, yet I suspect if you asked experts to list the so-called big hitters of the modern game, he wouldn't get a mention. He was courageous, too, with that inner strength to battle on and get the job done. He carried his bat twice in one-day internationals, and I well remember the quality of his unbeaten 126 against New Zealand in Chandigarh during the 1987 World Cup. Batting first, we were struggling a bit, but Swampy stuck at it and made the difference. He hit two sixes in the final over of the innings and Australia eventually won by 17 runs.

Few friendships in cricket have been stronger than the one between Swampy and David Boon. They had an almost telepathic understanding of each other and shared a sense of humour which often didn't require many words. During one stint on the sub-continent they both had incredible haircuts and went out to bat looking like the Sesame Street characters, Bert and Ernie. One of the few times Boon ever snapped on the field was when he heard an Indian player call Marsh a cheat; David really went for the jugular, so much so that political correctness demanded an apology afterwards. However, we were all secretly pleased that he stuck up for his mate.

Boonie tells the story of one tour when they were rooming together and Swampy, as usual, wanted to talk. Boon, immersed in a book, wasn't interested. So Swampy pestered him and kept trying to break his concentration. Finally, he grabbed the book and simply tore it up! 'Now what do you want to talk about Boonie?'

There was a lot more to Swampy Marsh as a cricketer than meets the eye, and no-one should underestimate what he did for the game as a player. And I can't help thinking how fortunate the Australian team is to have such a high-quality individual as its new coach.

When I retired in 1968, at age 31, to try and consolidate business interests with an eye to the future, I really thought my first-class career was over. I was a trained journalist, could earn a pretty good living and was happy to develop a new career after doing well in cricket. I've always looked forward to a challenge and the challenge for me then was to establish myself in business.

The prospect of returning to first-class cricket was always there, but, to be honest, didn't really appeal to me. NSW offered me the job as captain more than once and it became something of a standing joke with their selectors: 'You ready Simmo?' 'Not yet.' 'We'll ask you again next year ...' At one point, I was sounded out by Kerry Packer about his plans for a 'rebel' competition, but had no interest in signing. And I was genuinely surprised when the ACB approached me to captain Australia again, after WSC's raid on most of their leading players. Sir Donald Bradman was very persuasive at that time and, naturally, I was very honoured. I was still playing club cricket, scoring as many runs as most and enjoying the game. And Australia were due to play a series against India; I still considered myself a pretty good player of spin bowling, so it all fitted in.

In 1984, I was involved in developing my sports marketing company when I was approached by Dick Guy, chairman of the NSW selectors, to coach the state side. They were in a bit of a mess at the time — lacklustre performances and poor morale — which was sad to see. So I gave it a go and we won the Sheffield Shield two years in a row. Whereupon I was approached by Fred Bennett, then chairman of the ACB, to coach the Australian side. I was not entirely sure I could devote myself to that, but, after visiting New Zealand as assistant manager-cum-coach, I realised there was an awful lot of important work that needed to be done. Standards were dreadfully low and too many players did not seem to treasure the honour of playing for Australia. It was painful to see and I wanted to be part of the cure. As it turned out, I was appointed coach for two years and reappointed four times.

When I first took the job on I announced that I wanted to do it well enough to put myself out of a job. My aims were to restore 'old fashioned' values and pride in performance, and to re-establish a work ethic second to none in the international game. In a sense I did that in 10 years, but the longer I was involved, the more obvious it became that the structure I grew up in had gone forever and that a coach was always going to be part and parcel of Australian cricket.

Please don't tell me that coaches are not necessary at the top level — not while Greg Norman has a coach and Pete Sampras has a coach and every high achiever in every international sport knows they need help to maintain their excellence. The notion that Australian cricketers are too good for that sort of thinking was, and is, macho drivel. And if the players believe it, which very few do, they are deceiving themselves.

Critics over the years have channelled their dislike of me into arguments against the coaching of elite players. They have publicly announced their delight at the success of the Australian team and privately seethed at the thought that Simmo might get some of the credit. Hard luck. I am proud of what I have contributed and proud of the players who restored Australia's cricket pride.

One fairly recent development which does trouble me is the tendency of some people to rewrite history, to suggest that the Australian team's recovery was somehow inevitable and, perhaps most unjust, to minimise Allan Border's contribution to that recovery, and, in a sense, his contribution to Australian cricket as well. The fact that Australia has done well under the captaincy of AB's successor, Mark Taylor, is used by some as proof that Border's influence was somehow negative. I know the players do not believe this and neither could anyone dealing with the facts.

Border and Taylor are very different people who go about the captaincy in different ways. Border was a reluctant Test captain who gradually grew into the job, Taylor is a confident young man who desperately wanted to be Australian captain. And why not? Border took over at a difficult time with relatively little to build on; Taylor inherited an experienced and talented team with strength in depth. It is relatively easy to be a good captain when you have a good team, in fact I don't know of any great captain of the past who did not have a very good side around him.

I have tried to profile the Border I knew in chapter six. In most respects, he and Taylor were contrasts. Taylor loves the authority and the profile the captaincy gives him, he is a ready mixer and loves to hold court, rattling away at an enthusiastic rate of knots which used to catch a few unwary journalists with rusty shorthand by surprise. He is as relaxed in the role of captain as AB was once uncomfortable.

Taylor is a very good organiser who likes to get matters in strict order for team meetings and in that respect I found him very easy to work with. We would have a chat beforehand, sometimes along with vice-captain Ian Healy, and map out just what we felt had to be tackled. By the time the players became involved we knew just where we wanted to go. This was a bit different from AB, who did not like structured discussion much and tended to be instinctive and reactive. AB didn't like to plan too much, but he invariably responded very incisively to ideas as they cropped up.

Mark and I had a good working relationship. We did not agree about everything, but then we were not expected to hold hands and show a common front just for the sake of it. Some sections of the media liked to present a situation where Mark threw off the shackles of conservative Simmo and created a team in his own image, as if that was the reason for the series win over the West Indies in 1995. A load of rubbish. In fact, more of my ideas were implemented under Mark's captaincy than they had been under Allan.

I sometimes found it difficult to get Mark to be as critical of the batsmen as he was of the bowlers, which is natural enough for a batsman, I suppose. On that Caribbean tour, we were very hard on the bowlers, very demanding, but it was a devil of a job to persuade Mark to focus on the batsmen in the same way. It was not until after a bad Test in Trinidad that we were able to have a very open — and sometimes heated — discussion with the batsmen. And they produced their best and most responsible batting performance in the next, series-deciding Test. A bit of friction never does any harm — if you can arouse the passion of the players, agreeable or disagreeable, it often focuses them and brings out their best.

It is inevitable that comparisons will be drawn between Border and Taylor, but they should be based on the facts and not on a desire to push a pet theory. When AB became captain in 1983–84, he did not inherit a lot and inevitably took time to build an effective side during a period when other sides were quite strong — England with Botham, Pakistan under Imran Khan, the West Indies with a long list of tremendous players. AB never had the luxury of playing the West Indies when they were on the wane, but he did almost beat them when they were the most powerful team in the world.

Mark was fortunate to take over an accomplished side and that makes a power of difference. Back in the early '70s, Ian Chappell inherited a team which included players like Ian Redpath, Doug Walters, Keith Stackpole, Greg Chappell, Rod Marsh, Dennis Lillee and Ashley Mallett, and he had a bloke called Thomson looming on the horizon. Not a bad foundation for building a reputation. That was a quirk of timing, a stroke of luck which any captain deserves, but it is also an important factor to consider if comparisons have to be made. And there are other things that people making comparisons should think about. For example: think of 1995 — no-one has ever mentioned the fact that neutral umpires were involved for the first time in an Australia–West Indies series there; I am not saying for a moment it was a huge bonus, but it certainly did not hurt. Neutral umpires are not mistake-proof, but their presence does help to relax players. That, in itself, is a major breakthrough.

Comparing teams of different eras is a difficult exercise, interesting but never an exact science. There are a lot more factors than win-loss equations, a point which should not be overlooked by those who call themselves experts and want their comparisons to prove something.

In his first two years as Australia's captain, Mark Taylor has done a good job, and he will continue to do so. He deserves enormous credit for his leadership in the West Indies, and he has all the attributes of a successful captain, not least excellent communication skills. However, he must realise that his real test will come in his next 24 months, when the workload will be punishing and the Australian team will have to be rebuilt to some extent. I do not begrudge Mark one bit of the praise he has received. However I recall, as some seem to want to forget, that Allan Border played a lot of his international captaincy career in a time when Australians did not know where their next Test victory was coming from. Give every captain his due, but don't let anyone ever belittle the contribution made by Allan Border to Australian cricket.

Acknowledgements

Special thanks to Terry Brindle for his help with the writing of this book. I am also very grateful to Prime Minister John Howard for generously agreeing to contribute the foreword, and to Steve Waugh for writing the prelude. And thanks must go to my long-time friend and colleague Ian McDonald, the media manager for the Australian Cricket Board, for his support.

Thanks also to the photographers whose work appears in the book:

Australian Picture Library/All Sport: pages x, 18, 35, 39, 40 (both pics), 46, 58 (both pics), 59 (all pics), 60 (bottom), 61 (both pics), 62, 63 (all pics), 64, 80, 96, 130, 144, 154, 161, 162 (all pics), 163 (both pics), 164 (both pics), 165 (top, bottom right), 166 (all pics), 167 (all pics), 168, 176, 187 (bottom), 188 (all pics), 189 (all pics), 190 (both pics), 191 (both pics), 192. 204.

Patrick Eagar: pages 28, 33, 37 (bottom), 38 (all pics), 165 (bottom left).

Ern McQuillan: pages 6, 34 (both pics), 36 (both pics), 37 (top left, top right).

Clifford White: viii.

Front cover photography:
Main pic: by Tony Nolan (Sport: the Library)
Top left: Bob Simpson with Allan Border, Ashes tour, 1993 (Australian Picture Library/All Sport)
Top right: Bob Simpson with Mark Taylor, Jamaica, 1995 (Australian Picture Library/All Sport)
Bottom: Bob Simpson with Damien Fleming, Chandigarh, 1996 (Australian Picture Library/All Sport)

Index